HisPlan MyPlan

Roadmap to Your Purpose

Gerald Duran

HisPlanMyPlan.com

ISBN (Print):   978-0-9985448-0-9
ISBN (eBook):   978-0-9985448-1-6

www.geraldduran.com

www.hisplanmyplan.com

Table of Contents

Dedication

This book is dedicated to three important women in my life: My mother Mary Carmen, who sacrificed everything to provide for us while we were growing up, who continued to walk and grow with the Lord throughout her life, and who has demonstrated grace throughout life's trials and blessings.

My mother-in-law Sandy, who without hesitation accepted me into the family fold, has treated me as her own son, has demonstrated love, and has accepted me through thick and thin.

And last but not least, my wife Leslie. She is my partner and the love of my life. There is no one on earth that I am closer to than her. She has been the perfect wife and mother to our children Brandon and Alec. She is full of grace, always an encourager, and a prayer warrior. Those trying to do something great with their lives need God and a Leslie in their corner.

I'd like to also thank my son Brandon, and my son Alec who lives with Jesus in heaven. I couldn't be more proud of you both.

Introduction

D eep inside every one of us is a God-planted purpose. Remember when we were young? Boy, how we could dream. Anything and everything was possible. We could become the President of the United States, a superhero, a mogul, a celebrity, or a professional sports star. There were no barriers and nothing was off limits; if we could dream it, we could do it!

This book was written for four types of people who most likely self-identify as:

1. **The Set-Back:** Those who have been set back have risked much to experience success only to encounter great loss. In other words, things went suddenly wrong for you (hence the setback). Perhaps you have lost your business or job, your marriage has failed, or a loved one has died. Whatever happened, you have experienced a great crisis that has shaken you to the core. What now?

Many of us have chased our dreams only to face great disappointment. We might have tasted what we thought was success (lifestyle, marriage, businesses, careers, great health, relationships, and children) only to watch it all slip away. Perhaps life's unfair circumstances or poor personal decisions just happened. Life can be full of setbacks and delays that feel like denials.

If this is you, then you have spent much time looking in your rearview mirror, asking "What happened?" We tend to look toward the past to attempt to get back the "good ol' days." *Oh, if I could only go back.* The problem is this type of thinking keeps us from moving forward with our lives. Anyone who has risked pursuing their dreams has faced and felt disappointment, setbacks, and delays. Many wounded warriors have just given up and surrendered their dreams to the battlefield because the wounds are too deep and life hurts too much. When you talk to these people, you can see the ugly scars of hurt and disappointment.

2. **The Serial Loser:** You have risked, yet you have never experienced success. You live life struggling without ever having experienced the win. You are sick and tired of being sick and tired. You've never met that special person or experienced that wonderful career. You've never had anything worthwhile to lose. Someplace between your dream and your destiny … YOU GOT STUCK! There is nothing to even look back at. Life hurts.

3. **The Realist:** You have never risked. You played it safe. You never chased a dream. You never chased anything. You let everything get away. That special person, the career, the business, or the idea you could have had, you allowed your circumstances to determine

your future. You were, after all, just being realistic. You just never had the courage to attempt anything great in your life. You played it safe. Your pain is different, the pain of not attempting to become the person you thought you might be.

4. **The Successful**: You have taken calculated risks and managed life well. You have sacrificed much to achieve your goals. You are successful, and yet you feel empty. You had a great plan; it just wasn't His plan, so you lack purpose.

   If you are in the so-called "success" category, you probably have no idea that life is about to go horribly wrong. People are generally in one of three life stages: 1) in a crisis, 2) coming out of a crisis, or 3) heading straight into a crisis. It's easy to get so caught up in all of your success that you ignore that feeling of emptiness and lack of purpose. You might have tried to fill this emptiness with "stuff," but God has a way of allowing hardship into our lives to draw us closer to Him. All too often "success" people feel they are self-made, and unfortunately often worship their creator – themselves! "Success" people who haven't yet experienced a great loss lack a weathered grain, a beautiful patina polished by overcoming life's challenges. Like a freshly crafted table, they need finishing and the finisher of their faith is about to step into the picture.

The truth is, WE ALL have an inner desire for greater purpose in our lives. Something meaningful. Something that matters. God created winners, not losers. We can all win by successfully living God's plan and purpose for our lives.

Despite your past or present season, God has created you and me on purpose … with a purpose. You may have allowed your perception of what's possible to shrink, and as a result many of your dreams have remained buried under a mountain of caution, doubt, and fear. The big dream now seems too risky and unrealistic. How would you even begin? After all, your thoughts are of an earlier time, the foolishness of a fantasy, perhaps the same type of fantasy as winning the lotto. You might hope or dream, but you don't believe.

My mission is to help you resurrect God's purpose and plan for your life, not your plan. So who am I? A pastor or a theologian? First and foremost, I am a child of God, just like you. I'm not a pastor, nor have I been to seminary. Aside from being a husband and a dad, I'm a business guy. A serial entrepreneur. A CEO. For the past 30 years, I've been in the trenches, helping people like you reach their goals.

Ask yourself this question: what would you set out to accomplish if you had all the resources and knew you COULD NOT fail?

If you believe God actually exists, there's also a good chance you believe God created every human being as part of His plan … **WITH** a specific plan and purpose for each one.

Most believers will agree that God has a plan and purpose for each one of us, yet when asked what their specific plan and purpose is, regrettably … they can't tell you.

That's because most people struggle to define what will make them happy – the American dream, the ideal career, a relationship, a certain house, a car, a specific level of income or lifestyle. We all want to know "What will make me happy, and how will I know when I get there?"

When life has not worked out the way we imagined, it's natural to ask, "Why am I on the planet? Is this all there is? There must be more, right?"

So what if God actually has a plan and purpose for your life? Wouldn't you want to know what it is?

The truth is, God will begin to meet the desires of your heart as you pursue His plan and purpose. Closely examine these three truths that will change your life forever:

Truth #1 – God has a master plan and purpose for your life.

Jeremiah 29:11 (NIV) – "For I know the plans I have for you," declares the Lord, "plans to prosper you and not to harm you, plans to give you hope and a future."

Truth #2 – God will reveal His plan (for you) to you.

Psalm 16:11 (NIV) – You have made known to me the path of life; you will fill me with joy in your presence, with eternal pleasures at your right hand.

Truth #3 – No person or thing can stop His plan for you … Except You!

Psalm 33:11 (NIV) – But the plans of the Lord stand firm forever, the purposes of His heart through all generations.

Whether you are a believer, an unbeliever, churched, de-churched, or un-churched, God stands ready to prove to you that He exists, that He loves you, that He has a plan and purpose for your life, and that His plan will completely fulfill you. Furthermore, no person, event, or circumstance can stop you from fulfilling His plan, except you,

SHOULD YOU CHOOSE not to identify it, pursue it, and fulfill it.

God does not promise us life on easy street, however. Life with or without God will have many struggles. Trust me on this one. I've been around the block a few times and life hasn't been easy. Growing up was hard. I was raised in a home with an alcoholic dad. Life was messy. A constant embarrassment. Dad came home drunk most nights. There was always tension until he got home because we knew he'd be driving home drunk. He was a big tough truck driver, and sometimes he drove the eighteen-wheeler home. So we worried. Then when he came barging through our front door, drunk as a skunk, first we were always relieved that he made it, and then the evening's fireworks began. Life wasn't easy. But we all have our stories, right?

If you knew that God, who created not only you but this entire world, was offering to help you, would you let Him? God desires a relationship with you that will become stronger through your struggles. So will you accept God's purpose and master plan for your life?

Together, we will explore a set of personal development stages you must go through as you identify and fulfill His master plan and purpose for your life. You might find yourself in more than one of these stages at a time. Each stage is a good stage, and every stage is a growth stage. The names I have given each stage are merely for clarity.

Some disclaimers: This book is only the messenger, not the message.

I am only providing you with the information to help you identify and fulfill God's plan and purpose for you. None of this information is new. In fact, you did not even have to buy this book to get the information. It's all available in the Bible. That's where I got it. I have only arranged it in what I hope is a logical manner to help you better understand the Bible's message. The Bible is the authority here, not this book. As you understand the Bible, it becomes knowledge. Nothing will work until the information converts to knowledge.

The first six stages (chapters) of this book will help you set a solid foundation for your journey. Without these foundational principles under your feet, you are likely to fail. Stages 7 and 8 will help you get started identifying God's master plan and purpose for your life. Stages 9 and 10 deal with God's ability to provide everything you need to accomplish that goal. Wow! God thought of everything!

Expect the Holy Spirit to be your personal mentor as you read this book, helping you convert the information into knowledge you can use to fulfill God's plan and purpose for your life. God has put six words on my heart for you as you begin this amazing journey.

FEAR NOT. BELIEVE ONLY. GET READY.

The Big Idea

Introduction

Get these three truths into your spirit and the knowledge of these truths will change your life forever. Because of this, nothing is impossible. Matthew 19:26

1. God has a master plan and purpose for your life. Jeremiah 29:11
2. God will reveal His plan (for you) to you. Psalm 16:11
3. No person or thing can stop His plan for you …
   Except You! Psalm 33:11

Notes

Introduction

Stage 1
Inheritance: Our Family Benefits

L ike most people, I didn't come from privilege. But I knew there were many who were worse off than we were. If we were poor, we just didn't know it. We were the lower middle class. I grew up in a Hispanic neighborhood of hard-working people struggling to hold on to the little they had. We weren't poor poor, but we always struggled to pay our bills. Ironically, I grew up around privilege, and I liked it. I just wasn't part of it; I was just an outsider looking in.

As a kid, I went to a Christian school operated by our neighborhood church, Community Grace Brethren Church in Whittier, California. While the school was located in a rough part of town, it attracted what we in the neighborhood referred to as "the rich kids." The privileged. They had family benefits we didn't have. Back then the church preached that people of privilege couldn't be Godly with all that money, but they seemed pretty happy to me. One particular family seemed to have it all, the Gemmils. Their son Curt was one of my best friends. They had money. They had privilege. Mr. Gemmil was a successful lawyer, drove around in a limousine, lived in a country club neighborhood, and had a vacation beach house ... life was grand. I benefited greatly from my relationship with him and his family. They treated me wonderfully, I enjoyed the perks of being friends with them, but I was still on the outside looking in. They had family benefits, and I felt fortunate to be their friend.

What I didn't know at the time was that as a child of God, I also had family benefits. In fact, being a Christian kid seemed more of a liability than a privilege. We were taught lots of rules, just not about the family benefits. I'm guessing the religious stiffs running the joint where I served time as a kid (the Christian school), also had no idea that our Father in Heaven was loaded, that we had some family benefits and no one bothered to tell us! Call it a lack of knowledge. We didn't know about the Will or the Inheritance, so we lived beneath our privilege. Way beneath. But if Jesus came so we would HAVE life, ENJOY life, and have it in ABUNDANCE through Him, then why are so many people, including Christians, so miserable?

Why is there so much lack instead of abundance?

For too many Americans, life simply hasn't worked out the way they planned. The American Dream no longer seems possible. Sixty percent of recent college graduates are either unemployed or underemployed. Too many good people have lost their jobs and can't find new ones. Millions have faced foreclosure and some have even faced homelessness. We Americans, along with the rest of the world, are buried deep in debt, living month to month, and for too many, retirement seems unattainable.

While working Americans may feel fortunate to have jobs, remarkably, 70 percent of Americans hate them. In other words, they're glad they are employed, yet they can't stand what they do for a living. They have a job, not a career. They are unfulfilled and feel they were meant to do something greater than what they are presently doing.

But the fact is, the average American will spend more than 100,000 hours working in unfulfilling jobs, trying to reach a dream many believe is no longer possible because they see their careers as avenues to their dreams.

Some blame the government, the President, Congress, Wall Street, the rich, the Democrats, the Republicans, the Jews, the Muslims, the blacks, the whites … the illegal immigrants, and many are simply angry with GOD for their misfortune.

Because of the stress so many Americans are under, divorce rates continue to skyrocket to almost 50 percent. Experts report this number would be even higher, but because of the economy, many simply can't afford the cost of a divorce.

Do you want to know what is more troubling than the doom and gloom of our present circumstances? Even though 92 percent of Americans believe in God, most Americans (including Christians) do not realize He never intended us to live this way.

The truth is … **GOD CREATED EARTH TO BE A PARADISE FOR MAN.**

Though Adam and Eve sinned, bringing the curse of sin to planet earth, when Jesus died on the cross for our sins, He paid the <u>full price</u> so you and I no longer have to live under the curse. We are redeemed from the curse!

Galatians 3:13-14 (NIV) – Christ redeemed us from the curse of the law by becoming a curse for us, for it is written: "Cursed is everyone who is hung on a pole." He redeemed us in order that the blessing given to Abraham might come to the Gentiles through Christ Jesus, so that by faith we might receive the promise of the Spirit.

Jesus says that Satan came to kill, steal, and destroy, but He came so we could have a full and abundant life:

John 10:10 (AMP) – The thief comes only in order to steal and kill and destroy. I came that they may have and enjoy life, and have it in abundance (to the full, till it overflows).

What so many people (especially Christians) miss out on is that once we become members of God's family (when we repent for our sins and invite Jesus to become Lord of our lives), we become His heirs, heirs to an inheritance left to us by God Himself. This inheritance is news to many, including those Christians who think of being born-again as a life insurance policy to gain entry into heaven. But they completely miss out on the fact that God has an incredible plan and purpose for each one of us here on earth.

The fact is, most of us are just too busy struggling along in life to read about our inheritance in the Bible. If someone like Bill Gates, one of the richest people in America, included you in his will, making you his heir, would you not read the will? There is a word for a person who is simply too busy to take the time to read the will. Take a look at what Galatians says about this:

Galatians 4:1-7 (NIV) – What I am saying is that as long as the heir is a child, he is no different from a slave, although he owns the whole estate. He is subject to guardians and trustees until the time set by his father. So also, when we were children, we were in slavery under the basic principles of the world. But when the time had fully come, God sent his Son, born of a woman, born under law, to redeem those under law, that we might receive the full rights of sons. Because you are sons, God sent the Spirit of his Son into our hearts, the Spirit who calls out, "*Abba*, Father." So you are no longer a slave, but a son; and since you are a son, God has made you also an heir.

Again, when you accept Jesus as your personal savior, you become a member of God's family. YOU instantly become an heir. Through Jesus Christ, YOU have access to ALL He has made available to His family.

The Bible is God's Word to us. It lays out His literal will (what He wants us to do) and His covenant will, which details His inheritance for us here on earth and in heaven.

But if you don't make time to read His Word, you'll wind up living beneath your privilege. To accept and receive the full benefits of this inheritance, you must first read "The Will" (the Bible) to understand what God promises us, along with His conditions and instructions for gaining access to our inheritance.

Before we move forward, let's agree on four basics:

1. God is our Creator.
2. The Bible is God's Word.
3. God's Word (The Bible) is His will.
4. God's will NEVER conflicts with His Word.

If you are struggling with these four basics, go to God in prayer and study the Word. I am 100 percent confident that God will reveal these truths to you in a way only He can.

Galatians 1:11-12 (NIV) – I want you to know, brothers, that the gospel I preached is not something that man made up. I did not receive it from any man, nor was I taught it; rather, I received it by revelation from Jesus Christ.

Some do not believe God's Word is 100 percent accurate and true. They believe "in" God, yet they really don't believe Him or His Word. Some believe only parts of the Word are for us, but this thinking limits God's message to us. It's true, for example, that 1 Thessalonians was written to the Church of Thessalonica, not specifically "to" Gerald Duran. The entire Bible, however, was specifically written "for" Gerald Duran.

2 Timothy 3:16-17 (AMP) – Every Scripture is God-breathed (given by His inspiration) and profitable for instruction, for reproof and conviction of sin, for correction of error and discipline in obedience, [and] for training in righteousness (in holy living, in conformity to God's will in thought, purpose, and action), So that the man of God may be complete and proficient, well fitted and thoroughly equipped for every good work.

As you go deeper into learning from God's Word, you will find that it is your personal guide for navigating your journey, that it will always work, that God always keeps His promises, and that God's Word is forever.

Psalm 119:105 (AMP) – Your word is a lamp to my feet and a light to my path.

Isaiah 55:11 (AMP) – So shall My word be that goes forth out of My mouth: it shall not return to Me void [without producing any effect, useless], but it shall accomplish that which I please and purpose, and it shall prosper in the thing for which I sent it.

Numbers 23:19 (AMP) – God is not a man, that He should tell or act a lie, neither the son of man, that He should feel repentance or compunction [for what He has promised]. Has He said and shall He not do it? Or has He spoken and shall He not make it good?

Matthew 24:35 (AMP) – Sky and earth will pass away, but My words will not pass away.

Isaiah 40:8 (AMP) – The grass withers, the flower fades, but the word of our God will stand forever.

If you are not a member of God's family but you want to be, this would be a great time to join it. Here are some simple steps to salvation so you can begin your journey to identify and fulfill God's plans and purpose for your life:

1. **Repent – Ask God for forgiveness for your sins.**

    Romans 3:23 (NIV) – For all have sinned and fall short of the glory of God.

    Acts 3:19 (NIV) – Repent, then, and turn to God, so that your sins may be wiped out, that times of refreshing may come from the Lord.

2. Believe – Receive the free gift of salvation.

Ephesians 2:8-9 (NIV) – For it is by grace you have been saved, through faith—and this is not from yourselves, it is the gift of God— not by works, so that no one can boast.

John 3:16 (NIV) – For God so loved the world that he gave his one and only Son, that whoever believes in him shall not perish but have eternal life.

Simply pray the following prayer in faith, and Jesus will be your Lord!

"God, I repent of my sins and ask for your forgiveness as you promise in Acts 3:19. I believe that you sent your son Jesus to the cross to die for my sins. I also believe that Jesus has risen from the dead. I receive your free gift of salvation and I commit my life to following Jesus Christ as my Lord and Savior."

If you have prayed this prayer, welcome to the family of God. Whether you are a new Christian or a seasoned pro, you are ready to begin your journey to discovering God's plan and purpose for your life. The point of this chapter was for us to realize how easy it is for us to live beneath our privilege because we've missed what Christ won for us at the cross. Your understanding of this inheritance will begin to make more sense as you move forward in this book.

Before we move on, I want to give you one example of a biblical promise that is part of our inheritance package. Throughout the

Bible, God instructs us not to worry or be in fear. These are not His suggestions; they are His commands to us and He expects us to obey them. This is one that we will all struggle with. But know this, God will never ask us to do something He has not empowered us to do through His Word. What would you give to be free from worry and fear? Actually, there is not anything you can give to be free from worry and fear. But God has made a way for us to have victory over worry and fear through the power of His Word.

Until 1996, I battled worry and fear with my personal will power. As an entrepreneur, every week was a battle. I accepted this stress as part of being a CEO. Just tough it out, right? I was in my mid-thirties and had just sold my company and entered a partnership with a competitor to build one of the fastest-growing companies in America. Until that point, the Bible was just a book of rules, a list of dos and don'ts. We went to church. We prayed. God was a helper, but in my mind, I did most of the heavy lifting. My wife Leslie was pregnant with our second child Alec.

It was easy-street with our first son Brandon. Such a good boy. Almost perfect. With great anticipation, we looked forward to Alec to complete our little happy family unit. I had dropped my wife off for a doctor's visit and drove to my office to get a few things done. I wasn't there long before I received a frantic call from the nurse instructing me to get back to the doctor's office immediately. My wife had been given some bad news and I needed to be there. That day we found out that Alec was a child with Down Syndrome, that he had a major heart defect, that he might not make it, that his life would not be ideal, and that he wouldn't be the perfect son we had hoped for. Who hopes for anything less than perfect, right? No one hopes for Down Syndrome. No one hopes for heart defects.

The doctors let us know we could terminate the pregnancy. Though we were upset, not knowing anything about kids with Down Syndrome or heart problems, we knew immediately that Alec was God's gift to us and that we were about to begin a new journey, perhaps a wild ride. So with great fanfare, Alec was welcomed into the world and into our family. Our life changed dramatically; we entered a season of spending much time in and out of Children's Mercy Hospital in Kansas City. It seemed as if we lived there. Alec went through many heart surgeries. We never knew whether he was going to live or die. Our thoughts constantly teetered between life and death.

Balancing life was hard. Leslie and I juggled our jobs, both sons, along with home and hospital life. We were exhausted and very very stressed. I can remember being at a breaking point and pleading with God, letting Him know that I was at my wits end, that I couldn't handle all the stress of this season ... and then I heard His voice. That faint voice in my heart stated very clearly, "Then give it to me." That week I searched the scriptures for every verse I could find on stress and how to get God's peace. To my surprise, there were many. I read them and it was clear. I didn't have to carry the burden; I could surrender it to God and find peace that passes all understanding.

John 16:33. John 14:27. 2 Thessalonians 3:16. Romans 15:13. Philippians 4:6-7. Isaiah 26:3. I found the scriptures. I read them. Now the question was, did I really believe them? Sure I believed in God. But did I have the faith to actually believe His promises? Make no mistake; these ARE promises. Not sometimes He does, sometimes He doesn't. No maybes. Through His Word, God was offering a promise – to me! He wasn't going to force it on me. They were mine to accept, just like I had accepted Him as my Savior at a young age. So I decided to JUST BELIEVE. And for the first time in a long time, my wife and I had peace. The trouble was not gone, but the stress, worry, and fear were gone. Many times we'd take the burden back, finding ourselves back to square one, only to surrender it back to God and receive our peace once again.

What I realized was the Bible wasn't just a book of rules. It was a book of promises. God's promises to us. These promises were part of our family benefits package, part of our inheritance. Turns out, there are about 6,000 promises in there for us, a promise for every challenge and obstacle we'll ever face. Moving forward, I decided to no longer rely on my personal will power; instead, I was committed to Word power.

This is part of the inheritance God has made available to us. Ephesians refers to this as putting on the armor of God. This is not available to nonfamily members. Are you starting to see what I mean by inheritance? In Stage 6, we'll address how to have victory over worry and fear, but for now I want to whet your appetite for more of these great benefits God has made available for our journey here on earth.

The Big Idea

Stage 1 - Inheritance: Our Family Benefits

The inheritance is our family benefits package that instantly becomes available to us when we become members of God's family. It consists of 6,000-plus biblical promises and truths that we as believers now have access to. I refer to this as *The Will*. No matter what we go through on our journey, there are scriptures and promises detailing how we can have victory over any and all circumstances that we might face in life.

1. You get saved. You get an inheritance. Galatians 3:13-14
2. You either know your inheritance or live like a slave. Galatians 4
3. Whatever your circumstances are in life, see what the Word says about your situation. Psalm 119:105
4. Learn the Word's conditions and instructions for gaining access to your inheritance, God's promises for believers. 2 Timothy 3:16-17; 2 Peter 1:4

Notes

Stage 1 - Inheritance: Our Family Benefits

Stage 2

Source: Hearing from God

Before God can communicate to you what His plan and purpose for your life is, you'll need to be able to hear His voice. This is an important step in coming to know our purpose, connecting and communicating "two-way" with God. In this chapter we'll address these four questions:

1. Can you have a meaningful relationship with God if you don't communicate with Him on a regular basis?
2. Can you really communicate with God if you are doing all the talking?
3. How does God communicate with us?
4. What do we miss out on when we don't spend time with God in prayer and in His Word?

Connecting and hearing from God is vital to a very personal, healthy, and meaningful relationship with our Creator. According to Barna Research Group, the nation's leading faith and culture research organization, 70 percent of evangelical Christians who live in the United States cannot clearly identify God's plan and purpose for their lives. Now think about this: can the body of Christ (Christians) really function as it should if 70 percent of us are unaware of our function and purpose? What would happen to our physical bodies if our body parts were unsure of their function and purpose? Can you imagine what would happen if a hand thought it was an ear? Maybe that's where the sarcastic phrase "talk to the hand" comes from. Our physical bodies would be non-functional.

That's exactly what has happened to the body of Christ, the Church (Christians), because it's members – that's us – individually are unaware of our purpose.

So here lies the question: How and why has this happened?

The answer is really simple. As Christians, we fail to comprehend what we miss out on when we fail to spend time with God, reading and mediating on His Word and hearing from Him directly through that living Word, on a regular basis. A whopping 90 percent of Christians have missed out on having the kind of "two-way" relationship that God intended for us to have with Him. You see, only 10 percent of Christians read their Bibles on a regular basis. As a result of not hearing and learning from God firsthand, sadly, most of our information on or about God tends to be second- or third-hand information. Our perception of who God is, what He has already done for us, past, present, and future, are mostly based on this second- and third-hand information.

We have allowed organized religion to replace the Word of God and the Holy Spirit. How? Well, if you haven't invested time with God and His Word on a regular basis, then you have exchanged the voice of God for the voice of religion or even your pastor. Your perception of WHO God is, and WHAT He has done and will do for you is subject to the opinions of the religious leaders you listen to. Please don't get me wrong here; God calls pastors to disciple us and help us grow. But pastors are not substitutes for the Bible. In fact, Martin Luther dedicated his life to giving all of us access to the Bible.

If Jesus were alive in the flesh today and you were attempting to understand a Biblical truth, would you ask the disciples or Jesus for an explanation of the truth? You would ask Jesus, the source of all truth, right? So what has changed today? Once we become members of God's family, heirs to His kingdom, part of our inheritance is that the Holy Spirit comes to live inside us. The Holy Spirit is our personal teacher and mentor, our personal comforter and guide. When we invest time with God, reading and mediating on His Word, the Holy Spirit mentors and reveals biblical truths to us.

If you are following Christ as you pursue God's plan and purpose for your life, then hearing His voice is a must. If you struggle in this area, I would advise you to make sure you are spending plenty of time with God in His Word and in prayer. God desires two-way communication with us, but when we can't hear His voice, we simply miss out on much of what He has planned for us, and what He has generously made available to us through His inheritance for us. Remember, when you became part of God's family (by accepting Jesus Christ as your personal Savior and Lord of your life), you were included as a beneficiary to His will. You are entitled to ALL God wants us to have. Family benefits. Family privileges. As they say, membership has its privileges. Favor ain't fair; it's JUST.

Now, at this point you might be thinking, *Oh Gerald, that sounds like a prosperity message, not the suffering-for-Jesus message I grew up on.* Yes, it is true that we will suffer on our journey, but I've got news for you. Jesus didn't die on the cross so you could fail. He died on the cross so you could succeed. Jesus suffered and we'll suffer for victory. There is rarely a success without a battle.

The question is, succeed at what? Some would say, "There he goes again with that prosperity 'name it and claim it' teaching." No, those are your thoughts, not mine. The question is Godly success or worldly success? **The success I'm talking about is successfully fulfilling God's plan and purpose for your life. Nothing more, nothing less.**

When Jesus died on the cross for our sins and rose again on the third day, this powerful event was part God's plan to allow us as His children to gain access to family benefits. Sadly, this is news to many believers.

Most of us already know how to speak TO God; we call it prayer. It's just us talking to Him through our thoughts or out loud. When we pray, He's always listening. We can pray on our knees, in our cars, in the shower, at work, in church … any way and anywhere. God not only loves us, but He loves to hear from us.

So if praying is the way we communicate with God, how does He communicate with us?

Through The Holy Spirit – When we receive Christ as our personal Savior, the Holy Spirit comes and resides inside each one of us. This is that quiet voice speaking inside you and into your thoughts.

Through Other People – God often uses other people to speak to us. He may use a message from your pastor, friends, family, or even a complete stranger.

Through His Actions – God often uses His actions to communicate His message to us. The Bible is full of examples of God sending a message through His actions. He opens doors, shuts doors, disciplines us, and rewards us with His actions.

(NOTE: Of all our communications to God, our actions speak the loudest to Him.)

Through Dreams – God has used dreams throughout history to communicate with man.

Through The Bible – This is the primary way that God will communicate with us. When we spend time with God in the Word and in prayer, the Holy Spirit reveals His message to us. He teaches us deep insights and communicates God's fullest message to us.

While each book in the Bible wasn't written specifically to you and me, it was written specifically for us.

2 Timothy 3:16-17 (NIV) – All Scripture is God-breathed and is useful for teaching, rebuking, correcting and training in righteousness, so that the servant of God may be thoroughly equipped for every good work.

However God chooses to communicate with you, His message will NEVER contradict His Word. I have missed His message a few times when I have confused my feelings with the promptings of the Holy Spirit.

So beware, that feeling inside you may turn out to be the result of the chili you ate for lunch and not the Holy Spirit. Remember, we're continually hearing four voices in our heads: our thoughts, voices from the world, lies from Satan, and truth from the Holy Spirit. But through time invested in God's Word, you'll come to recognize the Shepherd's voice if you haven't already. This is a Biblical truth according to the following two scriptures in the book of John:

John 10:27 (NIV) – "My sheep listen to my voice; I know them, and they follow me."

John 10:4-5 (NASB) – "When he puts forth all his own, he goes ahead of them, and the sheep follow him because they know his voice. A stranger they simply will not follow, but will flee from him, because they do not know the voice of strangers."

When God is communicating to us, His message will be persistent, and He may send it through a variety of His communication channels. Many times when I've heard that quiet voice (the Holy Spirit) prompting me, I'm not at all surprised when I happen to read something in the Word that correlates with that specific message. Nor am I surprised when a friend or pastor shares a similar message. It seems that when God is speaking to me, I often get bombarded with the same message from many of God's various communication channels. So when you think God is sending you a message, take it to God in prayer. Just ask Him, "Lord, is this you?" Wait for His answer; it will always bring peace to you. Then act on God's instructions. Remember, God's message to us is persistent, it will always line up with His Word, and it will always give you peace to obey.

The genesis of *HisPlan MyPlan* began with my hearing the voice of God. Not audibly, but a persistent calling to build a curriculum of how to identify and fulfill God's plan and purpose for one's life. The *HisPlan MyPlan* curriculum began as my personal life success checklist. Over the years of being mentored to, listening to great preachers, and spending much time with God in His Word, the ten chapters of this book, representing ten critical stages for walking in God's will, began as my personal checklist. A spiritual how-to for dummies, with me being the primary dummy. I had stacks and stacks of journals and spiral notebooks containing everything I had ever learned from my studies of the Word. Lots of practical how-to's and what-to-do's. When my life would get out of balance, or I encountered trouble, or I stopped hearing God's voice … I looked to my notes for an answer. **My notes always pointed to specific scriptures and what I learned from them.**

HisPlan MyPlan also became the curriculum I used to mentor and disciple others. Because I was known as a successful business leader, people gravitated toward me throughout the years, for mentorship. When I brought up faith, they listened. Much of my time, energy, and money have been invested into helping hurting people who were struggling with life. It has always felt like an honor or a privilege when others reach out and share their very personal challenges, and to give me the chance to be part of their solution. The checklist was the center point for all my conversations.

In the late nineties, God began speaking to me about putting the *HisPlan MyPlan* message into a formal curriculum. I procrastinated and delayed. I reasoned with God that I am a business guy, not a preacher or a religious teacher. But His message to me was persistent: "Do it. Obey." At the time I was the president of an educational company. We had a curriculum department and I knew a thing or two about building a curriculum. But I felt so under-qualified to build some kind of faith-based study like *HisPlan MyPlan*. After all, a curriculum for whom? Who would read it? I didn't want to do it. But God wore me down, so I finally obeyed and began developing the curriculum.

Months later when it was finished, I thought, *OK, now what?* Then one Sunday the video announcements of the church I attended advertised a career and purpose seminar. The bullet points on the big screen sure sounded a lot like what I had written. So I decided I might volunteer. I met with the pastor in charge of the event and he asked me to teach the course. That led to many other teaching and mentoring opportunities.

Then God began speaking to me about building a curriculum the world could access. So I pumped some serious dollars into creating an interactive online video curriculum, HisPlanMyPlan.com. We had to purchase digital cameras and sound equipment, and figure out where we would shoot the series. Getting video to run on a private website was hard to figure out back then. This was pre-social-media. Today everything online is built for video but back then there were many challenges.

After about a year, our work was finished and the website went live. Only one problem! How would anyone find it? How would we market it? I had self-funded the building of the site and the buying of the video and audio equipment, but I didn't have the budget to market it. So I went back to God and asked, "Now what?" **I needed to hear His voice.** Then one afternoon God put an idea in my head. How did I know it was God? Because the idea wouldn't work without a miracle. At the time, my company was the largest buyer of radio advertising in the part of Indiana where I wanted to launch. The idea was that I would approach the radio stations and ask them to give me a free spot for every paid spot I bought for my company. So if I bought 30 expensive drive-time spots at $300 a spot, I wanted 30 more drive-time spots for free. Unheard of. I essentially asked them to give me $30,000-$40,000 a month in free advertising for HisPlanMyPlan.com. Trust me; they don't do that.

I pleaded with God that this idea wouldn't work, that perhaps God didn't understand marketing the way I did. So of course, every station went along with our strategy, which was basically, "If you want to keep our business, you must do this." The only station that balked was a national Christian station. Go figure. But I pressured them and they gave in too! Sometimes God plays hardball. We ran a 9-month campaign, 3,000 people went through our online course, and 150 people got saved the first month. This led to a year of live events in that city. All this to say, **you'll never get much done for God if you can't hear His voice.** God knows how to get things done. He's always talking; we need to be always listening.

So what do we miss out on if we can't hear His voice?

We miss out on two-way communication with God. We pray, He listens, He talks back, but we miss His voice. Why? Because many Christians have never connected <u>not reading the Bible</u> with <u>not hearing His voice</u>. And this has become a HUGE problem within the Body of Christ, the Church. Can you picture a football team where the quarterback could hear the players, but the players couldn't hear the quarterback? It would be tough to call and execute a play, wouldn't it? In fact, game day would be one ugly mess. Or, imagine a battle where the command center could hear from the soldiers, but the soldiers couldn't hear from the command center. Certain chaos leading to casualties and death. Well, guess what? If you are saved, you have joined the army of the Lord. Try getting anything done for God if you can't hear His voice. As Christians, we'd end up pretty ineffective, wouldn't we?

We miss out on a healthy relationship with God. Our Father desires a very personal relationship with us. If we can't hear His voice, we miss out on a healthy relationship with Him. Let's face it; it's impossible to have a healthy relationship with anyone, including God, if your communication is all one-way, (you're doing all the talking). I think we would all agree that one-way relationships are extremely unhealthy, and that any relationship or marriage would certainly fail if only one person did all the talking. That's not communication. We've all known someone who doesn't listen and only talks. You know, windbags. There's one in every family and plenty at work; they are everywhere.

I spend much of my time counseling Christians who are trying to identify God's plan and purpose for their lives. I often ask them to describe their relationship with God and then somewhere in the conversation, I'll ask them how much time they spend reading the Word and praying to Him. I'd say 80 percent of the time, I hear something like, "Well, not as much time as I should." Usually that's code for "Very little or none at all." Without being legalistic I ask you this question: if we desire a healthy relationship with God, how much time should we invest in two-way communication with Him? Not sure? It's really just common sense. How much time would you spend at the gym if you needed to get in shape? Would five or fifteen minutes get the job done for most of us? Oh I wish.

How about with God? At the end of the day, our results will be the evidence of the time invested. There are no shortcuts here; this is why we have priorities. God's priorities are simply amazing to me. God has carved out a 24/7 availability schedule for every person on the planet who desires to get to know Him and follow Him. It would do us well to consider this fact as we set our schedules to include time with Him.

We miss out on a healthy perception of God. Who is God? Without a healthy relationship with Him, can we really answer that question? Oh, we can repeat what we've been told about Him, but we can't really know who He is unless we have a healthy relationship with Him. And a healthy relationship only comes from investing time spent in two-way dialogue with Him.

Who is Bill Gates? We can all say "the founder of Microsoft," or "one of the richest men on the planet." But unless we've spent much time with him, our perception of him is only based on second-hand information. It might be gossip, lies, or the truth, but we wouldn't really know what to actually believe.

The truth is, God wants us to know Him. He wants us to have an accurate perception of who He is and His unconditional love for us. Our perception of who He is, His love for us, what's possible through Him, and His ways of doing things can get completely warped without proper perception. We can easily end up at the mercy of religious opinions, second-hand information, and outright lies from others who want to tell us what to believe. As a result, we end up with a plethora of opinions about things spiritual, but we're unable to back them up scripturally to know what is true and what is false. Our knowledge of God's truth will lack depth, and like a parrot, we can only repeat what someone else has told us, whether it's true or false. We can easily end up with religious information about God, but no personal knowledge of Him, which comes only by investing time with God in His Word.

Has there ever been a time when a particular scripture jumped right off the page at you while you were reading the Word? You may have read that scripture a hundred times, but this time, you received a deeper truth. In these special moments, we get revelation of the scripture's truth directly from the Holy Spirit. This is the revelation that comes from having a relationship with God. It's where religious information transfers to revelation knowledge, and it comes only from two-way communication with God Himself.

We miss out on having a strong faith. Life lived without faith is life lived in doubt, worry, and fear. Faith is central to receiving all God has promised us.

Hebrews 6:12 (NIV) – ...through faith and patience inherit what has been promised.

So why is having faith one of our greatest areas of struggle? I've often said with sarcasm, "We Christians don't have a problem believing in God; we have a problem believing Him." Look, even Satan believes God exists, but to follow Him, we need to have faith in Him and His Word. And in faith, our actions will match what we believe.

James 2:17 (NIV) – In the same way, faith by itself, if it is not accompanied by action, is dead.

So why is faith such a struggle for us? Because so often our faith is based on will power, not Word power. Faith isn't something we manufacture; it comes by spending time with God – in the Word, in prayer, and by doing what we believe.

Hebrews 12:2 (NIV) – fixing our eyes on Jesus, the pioneer and perfecter of faith. For the joy set before him he endured the cross, scorning its shame, and sat down at the right hand of the throne of God.

What an amazing system God has. First by faith, we have access to all God promises, and then God provides us with a process for developing that faith.

Romans 10:17 (NIV) – Consequently, faith comes from hearing the message, and the message is heard through the Word of Christ.

In fact, we can't please God without it!

Hebrews 11:6 (NIV) – And without faith it is impossible to please God.

The truth is, faith has been called God's currency to receive all He willed for us to have. In the book of James, for instance, we read how we can receive Godly wisdom by faith. Faith is the currency required for gaining wisdom, and without it, we cannot expect to receive anything from God. God is not moved to action by our need alone. If that were true, there would be no lack in this world; there would be no suffering or hunger. God has a system, His way of doing things.

James 1:5-7 (NIV) – If any of you lacks wisdom, you should ask God, who gives generously to all without finding fault, and it will be given to you. But when you ask, you must believe and not doubt, because the one who doubts is like a wave of the sea, blown and tossed by the wind. <u>That person should not expect to receive anything from the Lord</u>.

When we accept Christ as our personal savior, we are all born into Christ with a measure of faith. Faith is a spiritual muscle that needs to develop. This faith muscle is like the mustard seed; it may start out tiny, but when it grows, it can move mountains.

Matthew 9:29 (NIV) – According to your faith it will be done for you.

Mark 11:22-24 (NIV) – Have faith in God, Jesus answered. Truly I tell you, if anyone says to this mountain, "Go, throw yourself into the sea," and does not doubt in their heart but believes that what they say will happen, it will be done for them. Therefore I tell you, whatever you ask for in prayer, believe that you have received it, and it will be yours.

Life is miserable without a developed faith. Without it, we live beneath our privilege in doubt, worry, and fear.

We miss out on every Biblical truth and promise meant for us. The scriptures are an immeasurable deep well of God's truths, principles, promises, purpose, and will. It is our instruction book for life and abundant living. Through it, we get knowledge, wisdom, and understanding of God's will. His Word is literally His will for us. It is both what He purposed (what will come to pass), and His literal inheritance to us as believers – sons and heirs to His kingdom.

Acts 22:14 (NIV) – Then he said: "The God of our ancestors has chosen you to know his will and to see the Righteous One and to hear words from his mouth."

When I first began spending time with God in His Word, I realized the Bible was a book of promises, not a book of rules. The Bible became God's personal will to me, my inheritance. Only a fool is left an inheritance but does not read the will.

The Bible is where God makes the unchanging nature of His purpose clear. It is where we come to understand the certainty of His promise. Through reading the Word, we can come to understand that we are sons of God and that we have an inheritance. Until we know who we are in Christ, we live like slaves, not heirs.

Galatians 3:26-4:7 (MSG) – But now you have arrived at your destination: By faith in Christ you are in direct relationship with God. Your baptism in Christ was not just washing you up for a fresh start. It also involved dressing you in an adult faith wardrobe—Christ's life, the fulfillment of God's original promise.

In Christ's family there can be no division into Jew and non-Jew, slave and free, male and female. Among us you are all equal. That is, we are all in a common relationship with Jesus Christ. Also, since you are Christ's family, then you are Abraham's famous "descendant," heirs according to the covenant promises.

Let me show you the implications of this. As long as the heir is a minor, he has no advantage over the slave. Though legally he owns the entire inheritance, he is subject to tutors and administrators until whatever date the father has set for emancipation. That is the way it is with us: When we were minors, we were just like slaves ordered around by simple instructions (the tutors and administrators of this world), with no say in the conduct of our own lives. But when the time arrived that was set by God the Father, God sent his Son, born among us of a woman, born under the conditions of the law so that he might redeem those of us who have been kidnapped by the law. Thus we have been set free to experience our rightful heritage.

You can tell for sure that you are now fully adopted as his own children because God sent the Spirit of his Son into our lives crying out, "Papa! Father!" Doesn't <u>that privilege of intimate conversation with God</u> make it plain that you are not a slave, but a child? And if you are a child, <u>you're also an heir, with complete access to the inheritance</u>.

To learn God's master plan and purpose for your life, you must be able to hear His voice. So much is simply forfeited when we miss out the voice of God's Word.

The Word is never silent, nor is God.

Jeremiah 7:23 (NASB) – But this is what I commanded them, saying, "Obey My voice, and I will be your God, and you will be My people; and you will walk in all the way which I command you, that it may be well with you."

God is our King, our leader. He has a plan and purpose for each of us. To succeed in our journey to identify and fulfill God's plan and purpose for our lives, we'll have to prioritize and invest time with Him in prayer and studying His Word, the Bible. Our God makes Himself available to us 24/7. Communicating with Him is a choice we get to make every day of our lives.

The Big Idea

Stage 2 - Source: Hearing from God

You'll never do much for God or have a meaningful relationship with Him without hearing His voice. Miss this, and you will miss out on almost everything that God has planned for your life. Spending time with God in prayer, and in the Word, is essential to a healthy life. Without time invested in this area you will have a starved spiritual life. Miss this, and you'll miss out on most of the wonderful adventures, blessings, and rewards reserved for those who identify and fulfill God's plan and purpose for their lives.

1. Don't read the Bible. Don't hear His voice.

Notes

Stage 3

Permission: Changing the Way We Think

I n Stage 2 we learned the importance of having two-way communication with God so we can hear His voice. Now that you have begun the exciting journey of identifying and fulfilling God's specific plan and purpose for your life, I am going to ask you to stop for a moment and examine the way you think. Before you take another step, I want to help you avoid a HUGE destiny blocker.

If something inside you has kept you from reaching your destiny, let's expose it, eradicate it, and replace it with Godly wisdom so you can proceed with your journey to fulfilling what God has called you to do. Ask yourself these three questions:

1. If you had a "life manager" responsible for all your life results thus far, would you sign up for thirty more years under the same manager?

2. Aren't you, in fact, your life manager, responsible for all your life results thus far?

3. Do you want to continue under the same management, or is it time to fire you?

Tired of getting nowhere fast? Let's eradicate what's stopping you from reaching your destiny.

Have you ever met people who keep making the same mistakes over and over again, personifying that old saying, "Insanity is doing the same thing over and over again, expecting different results." It's as though they are simply blind to their own failures, and from their perspective they are only victims of their circumstances and not intentional participants accountable for their results.

You see, even though people around them can clearly see what they're doing isn't working, they simply ignore what is obvious to everyone else ... their lack of results. To make matters worse, almost as if their lack of results weren't enough proof, they keep on keeping on ... repeating this cycle of failure. They are in a rut but always seem to have circumstantial excuses explaining their lack of progress. Sadly, their excuses are only bridges leading to nowhere where they've been busy erecting monuments of nothingness. For some, this lack of progress is a lifestyle, and for others it's only a stage in life where they have become stuck.

Maybe as you read that rather harsh description, you thought of someone you know who fits it. Or maybe reading it touched a nerve because you discovered you are that very person.

The fact is most people who are struggling really want to change. They are tired of the lack of progress and fulfillment in their lives. Though some of these individuals might appear outwardly successful, inside they are miserable because they know they were created for some greater purpose; they just don't know what it is. So if they want change, what's stopping them? Stinkin' thinkin'.

The way we THINK determines what we DO, and what we do determines our RESULTS. To change our results, we must be willing to give

God permission to change the way we think, to renew our minds. Our thinking shapes our results.

Thinking > Doing > Results

We have to give God permission because He'll never force it on us. The renewal of our minds comes as we spend time with God in prayer and in the Word. This is where we GROW, from our way of thinking … to His way of thinking. We can't learn, grow, or change until we allow God to begin the ongoing process of renewing our minds.

Romans 12:2 (NIV) – Do not conform to the pattern of this world, but be transformed by the renewing of your mind. Then you will be able to test and approve what God's will is—his good, pleasing and perfect will.

Proverbs 3:5-6 (AMPC) – Lean on, trust in, and be confident in the Lord with all your heart and mind and do not rely on your own insight or understanding. In all your ways know, recognize, and acknowledge Him, and He will direct and make straight and plain your paths.

Ephesians 4:22-24 (AMPC) – Strip yourselves of your former nature [put off and discard your old unrenewed self] which characterized your previous manner of life and becomes corrupt through lusts and desires that spring from delusion; And be constantly renewed in the spirit of your mind [having a fresh mental and spiritual attitude], And put on the new nature (the regenerate self) created in God's image, [Godlike] in true righteousness and holiness.

Imagine you're in Los Angeles and headed to New York, and you have a GPS system loaded with mapping data from the 1940s. You would find yourself making many wrong turns, getting completely lost and frustrated. Your journey would not work out the way you planned. Operating life's journey without God's knowledge, wisdom, and understanding is the same as making a journey with outdated GPS data. When we make a commitment to follow God and learn His way of doing things, we have to allow Him to completely renew our minds. It's like updating our personal GPS with God's knowledge, wisdom, and understanding.

1 Corinthians 2 (NIV) – And so it was with me, brothers and sisters. When I came to you, I did not come with eloquence or human wisdom as I proclaimed to you the testimony about God. For I resolved to know nothing while I was with you except Jesus Christ and him crucified. I came to you in weakness with great fear and trembling. My message and my preaching were not with wise and persuasive words, but with a demonstration of the Spirit's power, so that your faith might not rest on human wisdom, but on God's power.

God's Wisdom Revealed by the Spirit

We do, however, speak a message of wisdom among the mature, but not the wisdom of this age or of the rulers of this age, who are coming to nothing. No, we declare God's wisdom, a mystery that has been hidden and that God destined for our glory before time began. None of the rulers of this age understood it, for if they had, they would not have crucified the Lord of glory. However, as it is written:

"What no eye has seen, what no ear has heard, and what no human mind has conceived" the things God has prepared for those who love him — these are the things God has revealed to us by his Spirit. The Spirit searches all things, even the deep things of God. For who knows a person's thoughts except their own spirit within them? In the same way no one knows the thoughts of God except the Spirit of God. What we have received is not the spirit of the world, but the Spirit who is from God, so that we may understand what God has freely given us. This is what we speak, not in words taught us by human wisdom but in words taught by the Spirit, explaining spiritual realities with Spirit-taught words. The person without the Spirit does not accept the things that come from the Spirit of God but considers them foolishness, and cannot understand them because they are discerned only through the Spirit. The person with the Spirit makes judgments about all things, but such a person is not subject to merely human judgments, for, "Who has known the mind of the Lord so as to instruct him?"

But we have the mind of Christ.

When we allow God to renew and reset our minds, our future won't be determined by our present circumstances. Instead, it will be determined by God's plan and purpose for our lives and our willingness to navigate life God's way, no matter the circumstances.

Instead of making decisions based on what we see and how we feel, we can learn to make our decisions based on God's vision and provision for our lives. Are you fully prepared to let God renew your mind so that you no longer lean on your old ways of doing things? This is a deliberate choice we must make. When we turned our lives over to God, we "committed" to follow Christ. Now we must commit to a new way of doing things – God's way.

Most people would agree that life is a journey full of peaks and valleys. How we navigate life determines our ability to achieve our dreams and goals. At some point, when we get tired of the results we've created, we have to fire ourselves and get out of the driver's seat. That means we have to be willing to set aside our judgment, wisdom, and knowledge (or lack thereof) and listen to God's. We will never have the capacity for growth until we are ready to do that.

When people or organizations fail to accomplish what God has set out for them to do, despite their good intentions, two internal reasons ALWAYS exist:

1. Pride/Ego – Refusal to admit the need for change. Before you can submit to the will of God, you must admit that your way of thinking and doing things doesn't work. If you can't do this, pride has set in, and **God will oppose you.**

   James 4:6 (NIV) – But he gives us more grace. That is why Scripture says: "God opposes the proud but shows favor to the humble."

2. Lack of Knowledge/Ability to Execute – Refusal to acquire the knowledge and ability that comes only by the renewing of our minds.

   My heart sinks each time I witness, or worse, allow myself to participate in stinkin' thinkin'. At my consulting firm RPM Strategic LLC, we do our share of business turnarounds for companies whose revenues have gone flat. These companies hire us to be the architects of their roadmap back to success. When folks like you and me, or even CEOs get stuck, the symptoms can manifest in various ways, yet the problem is always lack of knowledge. Life has a way of throwing us curveballs; perhaps the landscape shifts and we get sidelined or left behind. Why? Lack of knowledge. Hosea 4:6 says, "My people are destroyed for lack of knowledge." Rest assured that for every problem, God already has the perfect solution. God is never wringing His hands up in heaven, worrying to death because He doesn't know what to do. No matter what the problem is: financial, health, relational, or lack of purpose, God knows exactly what to do. And guess what? He is willing to share His solution for us, with us.

So what stops us from getting in-the-know? Pride and ego, which jade our perception of what's possible. We just can't admit that our way is broken, that we have stinkin' thinkin', and that we don't know how.

One of my fondest, but most difficult, relationships is with a CEO from Milwaukee, a repeat client. He originally reached out to us when his company was on the brink of failure. He had already laid off most of his team and his cash reserves were really low. What he was trying to do wasn't working. Our team examined his results, looked at what he was doing, and reached a solution that was obvious. What was harder for us to see was the thinking behind the mess, the stinkin' thinkin'.

He was very willing to <u>change what he was doing</u> so he and his company could succeed. We developed and executed a revenue acceleration plan and in less than six months we had exceeded our revenue goal. This was a big win. A huge success. And in only a few years' time, he had become very

very prosperous. Unfortunately, he only changed what he was doing for a short time so he could get the results necessary to get out of the mud. After that, the stinkin' thinkin' that sabotaged all his efforts to begin with reared its ugly head once again.

> Proverbs 26:11 (KJV) – As a dog returneth to his vomit, so a fool returneth to his folly.

> Proverbs 16:18 (KJV) – Pride goes before destruction, a haughty spirit before a fall.

> James 4:6 (ESV) – "God opposes the proud, but he gives grace to the humble."

> 2 Peter 2:22 (NIV) – Of them the proverbs are true: "A dog returns to its vomit," and, "A sow that is washed returns to her wallowing in the mud."

Those who adjust what they're doing, but not their thinking, always return to old habits. Five years later, for a second time, this CEO drove his company right back into the mud. By this time his company had expanded into multiple cities across the country, which multiplied his expenses, making the rescue ten times more difficult. We developed and implemented a revenue acceleration plan, and for a second time, his business was saved. He was thriving again, so much that he bought a beautiful five-million-dollar home in Florida, and once again he was enjoying the good life.

Fast forward five years and you guessed it, we received a familiar "help us" call. Same problem, just different circumstances. And for a third time, we rescued his business. This time was very painful. We had to close all his offices across the country except his headquarters, he had to sell his big house, and his leadership team took huge pay cuts. It was a long hard battle to get this company out of the red. We all worked many long nights and weekends to rescue it. The cost to everyone was enormous. But we did it.

A year later our revenue stream hit levels we never imagined. We produced more from a single location than he had ever produced from his multiple locations we had closed. You'd think this time, after all the loss, after the blood, the sweat, and the tears involved in turning this troubled company around, the CEO would have learned his lesson. But pride and ego kept him from admitting he was the big problem, that his stinkin' thinkin' was his greatest liability. As soon as we had turned this company around, yup, you guessed it, his stinkin' thinkin' re-emerged. I told this CEO I could see he was about to destroy everything his hard-working team had accomplished. We eventually fired him as a client. A year later the company was out of business. Why? Pride and ego. The CEO couldn't admit his way of thinking wasn't working.

We all know people who keep making the same mistakes over and over again, and after they get rescued each time, they swear they'll never make the same mistake again. But as sure as the sun will rise, they return to their old habits. Their folly. Their destruction. If that's you, just confess it to God, give Him permission to change your thinking, and get on with your life and accomplishing what He has created you to do. His plan.

I encourage you today to admit, submit, and commit to God's process for accomplishing His will, the renewal of your mind.

Give God permission and ask for His help – Tell God you want to give Him the remainder of your life to fulfill His master plan and purpose. Tell him you are ready for Him to completely renew your mind because you will fail with your current level of wisdom, knowledge, and understanding. Renewing your mind is just learning God's way of doing things.

Pray this prayer: "Dear Heavenly Father, Romans 12:2 commands me to be transformed by the renewing of my mind. Only then will I know what your will is. Also, Proverbs 3:5-6 tells me not to rely on my own insight or understanding, and Ephesians 4:22-24 says that when I commit to renewing my mind, I can become more like you. So I commit to follow you, and I ask you to begin renewing my mind so I can be transformed by you and learn your way of doing things. Thank you in advance for what I am about to receive. I pray this in Jesus' name, Amen."

The Big Idea

Stage 3 - Permission:
Changing The Way We Think

This is a simple rule: Anytime you're not getting the results you want, just stop. Then ask God to change your thinking (your perception of what's possible, and how God wants it done). Ask for a *God Idea* instead of settling for your so-called good idea. If you will do this continually, you'll soar across many valleys instead of walking through them.

1. When your results stink.
2. Ask God to change the way you think.

Notes

Stage 3 - Permission:
Changing the Way We Think

Stage 4

Learning: Developing a Learning Heart

As you continue your journey to identify and fulfill God's plan and purpose for your life, one thing is certain: you will encounter many problems and obstacles along the way. Perhaps you have already encountered many challenges and roadblocks, but you don't need to worry. Once we change the way we live (what we do), no problem or circumstance will be able to stop us from accomplishing what God set out for us to do. God promises to deliver us and give us the wisdom to accomplish His will. What is required of us is a learning heart so we can change the way we "do" and live.

Trouble is to be expected, but our delivery from ALL trouble is certain:

Psalm 34:19 (NIV) – The righteous person may have many troubles, but the LORD delivers him from them all.

The person with a learning heart can navigate through trouble:

Proverbs 1:5 (AMP) – The wise also will hear and increase in learning, and the person of understanding will acquire skill and attain to sound counsel [so that he may be able to steer his course rightly]

Wisdom is available to all who ask:

James 1:5 (NIV) – If any of you lacks wisdom, you should ask God, who gives generously to all without finding fault, and it will be given to you.

Nothing can stop God's plans:

Psalm 33:11 (NIV) – But the plans of the LORD stand firm forever, the purposes of his heart through all generations.

In Stage 3, we learned the importance of inviting God to completely renew our minds. Take note: God always renews our minds (the way we think) before He makes changes in our lives. But He'll never force this upon us. It will always be our choice to learn His way of doing things. Once we give God permission to change our thinking, the learning heart then creates the capacity for God to teach us to live differently.

1. If you are not satisfied with your personal results, do you have to change the way you do things?
2. Can you really change if you're not willing and ready to learn a new way of doing things?
3. Is it smart to limit what's possible to your limited past experiences?

Get ready to develop a learning heart so you can learn God's way of doing things, change your life, and become completely fulfilled.

When life hasn't worked out the way we planned, it's natural to want change. But to get that change we must to be willing to grow, and before we can grow, we must to be willing to learn.

Thinking > (Renew – Learn – Grow – Change) **Do > Results**

So what is the learning heart? It's the opposite of a prideful or stubborn heart. People with prideful or stubborn hearts haven't allowed God to renew their minds. As a result they are extremely slow to learn, grow, change, or experience God's best. Sadly enough, they settle for living beneath their Godly privilege.

The learning heart creates our capacity for growth in life. When we are ready to learn, we simply make room for God's knowledge, wisdom, and understanding – His way of doing things. Those with prideful hearts, however, can't admit that what they are doing isn't working when they lack the knowledge, wisdom, and the understanding to solve their problems. People who live this way function in a state of complete denial. It really is an unproductive way to live.

So, pride is what separates the person with a learning heart from the person with a stubborn heart. And God hates pride!

Leviticus 26:19-20 (MSG) – And if none of this works in getting your attention, I'll discipline you seven times over for your sins. I'll break your strong pride: I'll make the skies above you like a sheet of tin and the ground under you like cast iron. No matter how hard you work, nothing will come of it: No crops out of the ground, no fruit off the trees.

Proverbs 18:12 (NIV) – Before his downfall a man's heart is proud, but humility comes before honor.

Proverbs 16:5 (NIV) – The Lord detests all the proud of heart. Be sure of this: They will not go unpunished.

Daniel 5:20 (NIV) – But when his heart became arrogant and hardened with pride, he was deposed from his royal throne and stripped of his glory.

When someone who has a learning heart encounters a stubborn problem, they are quick to admit they can't solve the problem without God's help and immediately turn to Him for the answer. That person's humility allows this to transpire without delay.

Prideful people, on the other hand, can't take criticism without becoming defensive because they are insecure about who they are in Christ. They are easily threatened and their egos won't allow them to trust someone who might actually be trying to help them. They feel persecuted, and as a result, they surround themselves with cheerleaders and "yes" people. Do you know anyone like this?

Several years ago I took up golf as a way to spend time with my family. The ups and downs of golf remind me of life's challenges. If the ball doesn't go where I want it to go, at some point I just need to admit there is a problem with my golf swing, and more importantly, that I don't know how to correct it. My scorecard will always reveal the truth of my ability. (Trust me on this. If you have a pride problem, just take up golf and you'll be humble in no time at all.) You can buy the best golf clothes, golf clubs, and golf balls; you can join the most exclusive golf club in town, but if you have a problem with your swing, that little ball will not go where you want it to go. I guess you can always become what I call a "faith golfer," someone who calls what is not as though it were (in other words, a cheat). Or, just don't keep score and ignore the obvious, which I have done many times.

Several years back when I started playing the game, the first thing I did was buy all the best golf equipment. I ended up losing so many golf balls that my friends joked about following me on the course just so they could get free expensive golf balls. But after my first few rounds of golf I realized I had a problem – I stunk. At first I tried to fix myself on the golf range, swinging and sweating over thousands of range balls. What a waste of time. Then I wised up and took some private lessons from a real golf pro at an exclusive private golf club that I probably couldn't afford to join. The club allowed the golf pro to teach outsiders, however.

I was really nervous when I arrived for my first lesson. I think the members could tell I didn't belong. The guy at the pro shop told me to take a cart and then pointed me to the golf range to find the pro. People kind of looked at me like I might actually be stealing the cart but I drove to the range to meet the pro. His nickname was "Smoothie," and after I watched him hit the ball, I knew exactly why people called him that. He asked me to hit a few balls to demonstrate my swing, and of course, these happened to be the worst and most embarrassing shots I'd ever made. The sweat on my golf shirt showed how nervous I was. I'm not a small guy so sweating comes pretty easy for me; it was really bad that day!

The most comforting words I've ever heard came next. He said, "Gerald, you have a great athletic stance and I see your problem; fixing it is going to be easy." Wow, what a relief. I wasn't doomed to be golf's worst duffer after all. Smoothie showed me a few corrections and I began to hit those golf balls straight and long almost every time. The golf range was busy on that particular day, and Smoothie instructed me to look down the line of golfers on the range. He began pointing out each golfer's swing problem as we watched their balls slice to the right or hook to the left. Then he gave me a great compliment: "Gerald," he said, "most of these guys have been playing for years, and many of them have the potential to be great amateur golfers, but pride keeps them from admitting they have a problem they can't fix." To this very day when I am confronted with a stubborn problem I can't seem to solve, I am quick to remember Smoothie's reassuring words, "this is going to be easy." I can actually picture God saying that to me, that even though my problem may seem impossible for me, solving it is easy for Him. That makes it easy for me to admit I have a problem I can't solve, and quick to ask for God's help. God gave us the Holy Spirit to be our helper and comforter. So why would we operate without the gift God has freely given us – His Holy Spirit? One ugly word comes to mind, PRIDE.

You see, developing a learning heart comes easy if you can only admit that what you are doing isn't working, and that you lack the knowledge or ability to solve the problem without God's help. It's really that simple! But a spirit of pride will stop us dead in our tracks.

If you own a business that is unprofitable and nothing seems to work no matter what you try, just admit to God that you have a problem you don't know how to fix. Simple! If you pastor a church that isn't reaching the unchurched, just admit that you have a big problem you cannot solve without additional knowledge. If you have never been financially free, it's not that you can't; it's just that you don't know how. God is ready to help you. Just commit to becoming a learner!

Hosea 4:6 (NIV) – …my people are destroyed from lack of knowledge.

Our "reality" (what we think is possible) dramatically changes with a learning heart. When we are stuck, it's because we've set up stubborn boundaries or invisible fences to define what we believe is possible, thinking, *I'm just being realistic.* When we do this, however, we are actually operating in our limited view of what's possible, not God's view. We are allowing our limited past experiences to determine our future.

In my business of providing CEOs with corporate turnaround and revenue growth strategy services, I've always found the brightest and most successful CEOs were those who were quick to call us for help when they didn't get the results they were after. They'd say something like, "Gerald, sales at our Dallas office have tanked. We've tried everything we know, but to no avail. I need you to fly down there, figure out what's wrong, and fix it." These successful people knew exactly what they wanted and were quick to ask for help when they couldn't solve their own problems. That's because they have learning hearts.

Many pastors struggle with this. They lack the strategy to recruit, develop, and multiply their churches. Research from one of the leading religious research organizations shows that only 1 percent of the church is reaching the unchurched. Seems like a huge problem to me! I mean if changing the size of heaven is the absolute mandate of the church, then something isn't working. Pastors who have learning hearts ask for help in developing strategies to reach the lost, hurting, and unchurched. But too many others are simply in denial. The same research indicated that more than 80 percent of pastors lacked a written strategy and plan to reach the unchurched. Now, what does that say about being intentional? As they say, fail to plan, plan to fail. We all must have learning hearts if we want to fulfill God's calling on our lives.

Whether you are a CEO, a pastor, or just an average person like me experiencing everyday problems, obstacles, and challenges, we must be willing to admit when we have encountered a problem we cannot solve. Then we must be equally quick to turn to God for the knowledge necessary to bust through the obstacles that have blocked us from achieving what God has called us to do.

When you allow God to develop the learning heart within you, anything and everything becomes possible: becoming financially free, loving again, mending broken fences, solving your business problems, and even filling every seat in your church … ALL things become possible.

Philippians 4:13 (NIV) – I can do all this through him who gives me strength.

Matthew 19:26 (NIV) – Jesus looked at them and said, "With man this is impossible, but with God all things are possible.

Mark 9:23 (NIV) – 'If you can'?" said Jesus. "Everything is possible for one who believes.

Three Keys to Developing a Learning Heart:

1. **Learn the difference between problems and symptoms.** Most of the time, what we believe to be problems are only symptoms of our problems. Don't waste your time trying to fix symptoms; if you do, your problem never goes away. This will save you years of frustration and perhaps a ton of money.

    Lack of knowledge will always be your problem. Whatever you perceive your problem to be, the real problem is always you simply don't know how. Now those are fighting words for prideful people! If you know how, just fix it. See, if you could have, you would have, but you didn't. That's why you still have the problem. Remember, God hates and opposes pride.

Example: "My problem is that I am overweight." No, being overweight is just a symptom of the problem. The problem is not having the diligence to eat and exercise right.

Example: "My problem is that I don't make enough money." No, not having enough money is just a symptom of the problem. The problem might be not having the Godly knowledge, wisdom, and understanding to achieve your financial goals.

2. **Admit that you are where you are by choice.** These may be bad choices, but nevertheless, our choices. Ouch! Now listen, I'm not saying you chose the bad things that have happened to you. Bad things do happen to good people. No one chooses to be molested, stolen from, or taken advantage of, for example. But how you choose to respond to life's obstacles is always your choice. Your problem can actually become a learning moment in your life that will refine you, or you can simply let it define you as a victim for life.

Until we come to terms with this truth, we are victims and we are trapped. And by the way, choosing to do nothing is making a choice. Only when we admit that our future is only an outcome of our present choices and decisions do we become empowered to make the right choices for incredible change in our lives. Life's circumstances are NEVER a match for God's promises. We are deeply rooted in pride when we think our circumstances are too big for God to solve. We must stop blaming our lack of progress on our circumstances. If your mama dropped you on your head when you were twelve, and now you're forty-five, it's time to get over it!

3. **Be ready to allow God to help you His way, not your way.** When we have problems, we tend to plead with God for His help, and then proceed to tell Him exactly when, how, and what He needs to do to fix everything. In other words, we go to God and then take matters into our own hands, doing things our way and in our time frame. Or worse, we attempt to fix the problems ourselves. We've all been guilty of using both these methods to try to fix our problems.

Throughout my many years in the corporate turnaround consulting industry, the CEOs who hired us often begin giving us advice on how to fix the problems they couldn't solve themselves. Our response is usually something like, "Well, if you really knew how to fix the problem, why would you hire us?" Or my favorite, "If you could have, you would have, but you didn't, and that's why we are here."

Self-fixing makes as much sense as me trying to tell my golf pro how he should teach me to swing. Can you imagine me getting a golf lesson with one of the great professional golf teachers only to begin giving him instructions in the middle of the lesson on how to fix my bad swing?

Ultimately, the learning heart has an "I can admit I don't know how, but I'm willing and ready to learn" attitude that makes room for important change.

A stubborn heart has an "I'm just being realistic; if I haven't done it, then God can't do it" attitude that limits our future to our past experiences. Psalm 34:17 sets the bar for having a learning heart, turning to God for help first instead of last. For those with learning hearts, God is their steering wheel, not their spare tire.

Psalm 34:17 (NIV) – The righteous cry out, and the LORD hears them; he delivers them from all their troubles.

The Big Idea

Stage 4 - Learning:

Developing a Learning Heart

We will all face problems and challenges in life. This big question is whether we will try to self-fix (prideful) or God-fix (humble). This all depends on whether we have a *Learning Heart* or not. The person with a learning heart will choose to God-fix every time.

1. Ask God to change your *thinking*.
2. Ask God to change your *doing*, by showing you HOW He wants you to proceed.

Notes

Stage 5

Battle: Conquering Your Circumstances

The trouble with trouble is that it's inevitable. If you are alive and breathing, it's either coming or it's already here. It arrives via your circumstances and it can come out of absolutely nowhere. No one is exempt and no part of your life is off limits.

One day life seems great and the next day you've lost your job, or the doctor reports that you have cancer, or perhaps you learn your spouse wants a divorce. Experience has taught me that we are usually in one of three seasons in life:

1. In a crisis
2. Coming out of a crisis
3. Heading directly into a crisis, unbeknownst to us, even though everything seems fine

In Stage 4, we learned how to develop a learning heart so we could grow and change. In this stage, we will learn how to conquer our circumstances using God's Word, the armor of God.

We will explore:

1. Who's behind all the trouble
2. Why God allows it
3. How God expects us to respond to trouble

This is where you put what you have learned into action, confronting and conquering life's circumstances and problems God's way.

In my early entrepreneurial years, I used to pray that God would remove trouble from my path. I'd pray "Oh Lord, just give me one year with NO trouble; let me just cruise for a year, Lord, PLEASE!" I thought if I were obedient, if I could just be good enough, then God might remove all these challenges from my life. Well, He didn't. I thought a prosperous life was one without trouble. I was wrong. Living a prosperous or abundant life is learning how to conquer trouble through God's Word and His promises over our lives.

I started my first company in my early twenties. I was young and dumb, full of ideas, and short on cash. I had an abundance of trouble. At this early age I wasn't exactly living for Christ, but God was in my life and He was always rescuing me from trouble. When you start a business when you're young and dumb, you can be certain that much of your trouble will be financial.

The truth is, I have faced financial challenges most of my life. Yet my personal income has been in the top 5 percent of earners in America. How is that possible? You see, trouble is a set of circumstances that Satan has designed to destroy you. Whether or not your trouble is self-inflicted, Satan is always behind it. God, however, will use your trouble and present circumstances (if you invite Him to help you) to propel you forward in your journey. Resistance is how we develop our faith muscle. It's how God grows our faith. Trouble is really a setup for success.

Once God showed me this, I learned that lemons (aka trouble) were the key ingredients to making lemonade. So when life gave me lemons, I opened my first lemonade stand ... metaphorically speaking. Since then and with God's help, I've built many companies for myself and for my clients with this knowledge and perception of what trouble is ... and who's behind it.

Trouble is Inevitable. Expect Battles. Always Expect Victories.

As we progress on our journey to identifying and fulfilling God's plan and purpose for our lives, we will most certainly encounter troubling circumstances. Some will be slight and some severe. Some will be momentary and some will develop into lengthy seasons of tribulation. But we can also be certain that no trouble will take God by surprise and that God is always in control. He is with us every step of our journey. We are never left alone to deal with our troubles. We can be certain that no trouble or circumstance can stop us from accomplishing what God has called us to accomplish for Him. Our future is not determined by our present circumstances; our future is determined by God's plan and purpose for our lives.

When trouble hits home, everything can ever so suddenly seem less certain. It then becomes pretty easy to begin to have doubts about God's plan and intentions for us. Satan will rear his ugly head with all sorts of accusations and condemnation, and if we listen to it, we will lose hope and stop moving forward. Proverbs 13:12 speaks to this:

Proverbs 13:12 (NIV) – Hope deferred makes the heart sick, but a longing fulfilled is a tree of life.

In these moments, it is so important for us to be reminded of God's original intentions for man. God never changes and He has always wanted the best for us. God's blessing was more than a polite gesture after a sneeze.

Genesis 1:26-31 (NIV) – Then God said, "Let us make man in our image, according to our likeness; and let them rule over the fish of the sea and over the birds of the sky and over the cattle and over all the earth, and over every creeping thing that creeps on the earth." God created man in His own image, in the image of God He created him; male and female He created them. God blessed them; and God said to them, "Be fruitful and multiply, and fill the earth, and subdue it; and rule over the fish of the sea and over the birds of the sky and over every living thing that moves on the earth." Then God said, "Behold, I have given you every plant yielding seed that is on the surface of all the earth, and every tree which has fruit yielding seed; it shall be food for you; and to every beast of the earth and to every bird of the sky and to every thing that moves on the earth which has life, I have given every green plant for food"; and it was so. God saw all that He had made, and behold, it was very good.

What do you do when trouble comes? How do you recover when your life seems to be skidding out of control? Again, as children of God, our future is not determined by our present troubles or circumstances; it is determined by God's promises for our lives and our willingness to accept them. Once we fully understand and accept that reality by faith, our dreams (God's plan and purpose for our lives), our goals, our plans, our decisions, and our reality are now based on the truth of the Word, not on our circumstances.

I've never denied that trouble has existed in my life; I deny it's right to destroy me.

As a child of God, you have rights (God's promises), and the Word (God's will) is full of His promises to you. As Christians, these promises are His inheritance to us. The Bible is literally God's will for us. But unless we know His promises, we'll never know our rights as Christians. If you know how to hear from God (Stage 2), and you've invited God to change the way you think (Stage 3), and you have asked God to change how you live and what you do (Stage 4), you are now ready to conquer your circumstances step by step.

John 10:10 lays out the mission of Satan vs. Jesus:

John 10:10 (ESV) – The thief comes only to steal and kill and destroy; I came that they may have life, and have it abundantly.

Ephesians 6:12 reminds us that our battles are not against flesh and blood. This is why a flesh solution won't work. Our struggles are always spiritual battles requiring a God solution, a Word solution.

Ephesians 6:12 (NIV) – For our struggle is not against flesh and blood, but against the rulers, against the authorities, against the powers of this dark world and against the spiritual forces of evil in the heavenly realms.

Adam and Eve's battle wasn't with the serpent. It was with the devil that possessed the serpent. Trouble is only the front man for LACK – lack of finances, lack of health, lack of relationship, and lack of purpose. Most of life's troubles will fall into one of these four areas of lack. It is vital to realize who the terrorist is behind your struggle. We all know that life is full of peaks and valleys. As Christians, we can expect to encounter much trouble, but we <u>should expect</u> to attain <u>victory every time</u>.

What does the Word say about your trouble?

Psalm 34:19 (NIV) – The righteous person may have many troubles, but the Lord delivers him from them all;

1 Peter 4:12-13 (NIV) – Dear friends, do not be surprised at the fiery ordeal that has come on you to test you, as though something strange were happening to you. But rejoice inasmuch as you participate in the sufferings of Christ, so that you may be overjoyed when his glory is revealed.

Your trouble is temporary.

1 Peter 1:6 (NIV) – In all this you greatly rejoice, though now for a little while you may have had to suffer grief in all kinds of trials.

2 Corinthians 4:16-18 (NIV) – Therefore we do not lose heart. Though outwardly we are wasting away, yet inwardly we are being renewed day by day. For our light and momentary troubles are achieving for us an eternal glory that far outweighs them all. So we fix our eyes not on what is seen, but on what is unseen, since what is seen is temporary, but what is unseen is eternal.

God promises to be with you.

2 Corinthians 1:3-4 (NIV) – Praise be to the God and Father of our Lord Jesus Christ, the Father of compassion and the God of all comfort, who comforts us in all our troubles, so that we can comfort those in any trouble with the comfort we ourselves receive from God.

Why does God allow trouble?

First, no trouble can come to us without God allowing it. He allows it because the fight is fixed, meaning God knows in advance how He will use our troubles to make us better. Because God loves us as His children, He already has a faith-building solution to deliver us from ALL of our troubles and circumstances. God uses our troubles as a vehicle for us to grow and to be prepared for the next stage of our journey. The testing of our faith is the only way we can begin to understand that all things are possible through Christ. When we come to terms with the power of the Word and the promises of God, we learn how to completely trust God.

Trouble produces perseverance, perseverance produces character, character produces hope, and hope produces God's appointments.

Tribulation > Perseverance > Character > Hope > God's Appointments

In the past, every time I read James 1:2, I always wondered why any reasonable person would consider trouble pure joy. Really? Once I realized that trouble and tribulation are the "entrance" or the "driveway" to God's appointments, my perception of trouble changed.

James 1:2 (NIV) – Consider it pure joy, my brothers and sisters, whenever you face trials of many kinds,

Romans 5:3-5 (NIV) – Not only so, but we also glory in our sufferings, because we know that suffering produces perseverance; perseverance, character; and character, hope. And hope does not put us to shame, because God's love has been poured out into our hearts through the Holy Spirit, who has been given to us.

Even Jesus had to "learn" trusting obedience through what He suffered.

Hebrews 5:8-10 (MSG) – While he lived on earth, anticipating death, Jesus cried out in pain and wept in sorrow as he offered up priestly prayers to God. Because he honored God, God answered him. Though he was God's Son, he learned trusting-obedience by what he suffered, just as we do. Then, having arrived at the full stature of his maturity and having been announced by God as high priest in the order of Melchizedek, he became the source of eternal salvation to all who believingly obey him.

How do we survive trouble but also thrive as a result of it?

2 Corinthians 1:4 (MSG) – All praise to the God and Father of our Master, Jesus the Messiah! Father of all mercy! God of all healing counsel! He comes alongside us when we go through hard times, and before you know it, he brings us alongside someone else who is going through hard times so that we can be there for that person just as God was there for us. We have plenty of hard times that come from following the Messiah, but no more so than the good times of his healing comfort—we get a full measure of that, too.

The following is a tactical and a biblical step-by-step approach. But here's a BIG HOWEVER: Our feelings usually lag behind our faith. In other words, we might agree with the Word, but sometimes at the beginning of a faith battle, our feelings take a while to catch up with our faith. That's why I refuse to let my feelings into my cockpit. Feelings can be inaccurate, irrational, up and down, and subject to change. They are not trustworthy. God never changes and neither does His Word. So if you are presently going through some tough circumstances as you read through this, please note that Stage 6 of this book deals with managing your feelings and the highs and lows of your faith.

While intellectually, this step-by-step approach will make sense, emotionally your flesh will fight it.

Step 1 – Search the Word, identify every scripture pertaining to your circumstance, and learn your rights (God's promises) as a child of God concerning your problem. **Write these scriptures down** so you have easy access to them. Ask God to fill you with His wisdom, knowledge, and understanding concerning your situation. The goal is to get an "aerial view" of your circumstances … A GOD VIEW. God actually promises to answer our prayers.

John 16:23-24 (NIV) – In that day you will no longer ask me anything. Very truly I tell you, my Father will give you whatever you ask
in my name. Until now you have not asked for anything in my name.
Ask and you will receive, and your joy will be complete.

Mark 11:24 (NIV) – Therefore I tell you, whatever you ask for in
prayer, believe that you have received it, and it will be yours.

John 15:7 (NIV) – If you remain in me and my words remain in you,
ask whatever you wish, and it will be done for you.

Your perception of your circumstances will actually frame your results. What's bigger, your trouble or your God? Big perception of God =
big dreams = big goals = big plans = big action = big results.

Perception > Dreams > Goals > Plans > Actions > Results

Step 2 – Present your problem to God in prayer (ask and receive
forgiveness if your situation is self-inflicted), present the identified scriptures to God that by faith you will stand on and believe in. Write down
your prayers using scripture throughout as though you were a lawyer
citing case law. When you pray, you should stand on the Word of God. If
you don't, Satan will clobber you with doubt, fear, and worry before you
even finish your prayer, and you'll end it with "Oh, never mind."

Step 3 – Receive by faith God's promises over your situation even
if your circumstances remain unchanged. When you see a promise in
scripture:

1. Read it.
2. Decide if you believe it.
3. Receive the promise by faith.
4. Speak it.
5. Consider it done.

Step 4 – Begin and continue to thank God for answered prayer in advance. Somewhere between the promise and the payoff is a process. You have now entered the process. You'll have to commit to trusting God for the how and the when. Many times when we pray, we have a very specific idea of just how and when God needs to answer our prayers. But God is not our genie or our puppet. He will always use the situation to make us stronger. If He needs to teach you patience, you'll learn patience. Always ask God what He wants you to learn and what He wants you to do.

Step 5 – Develop an expectation of God fulfilling His promises. Never allow a mental picture of failure or anything contradictory to His Word to remain in your mind. Give your fear, worry, and doubt over to God. He has the shoulders for the load; you don't.

Philippians 4:6 (AMP) – Do not fret or have any anxiety about anything, but in every circumstance *and* in everything, by prayer and petition (definite requests), with thanksgiving, continue to make your wants known to God.

2 Corinthians 10:5 (NIV) – We demolish arguments and every pretension that sets itself up against the knowledge of God, and we take captive every thought to make it obedient to Christ.

1 Peter 5:7 (NIV) – Cast all your anxiety on him because he cares for you.

Psalm 55:22 (NIV) – Cast your cares on the Lord and he will sustain you; he will never let the righteous be shaken.

Step 6 – Begin the fight of faith with patience, expectation, peace, and perseverance.

We will be at the mercy of our circumstances until we learn to conquer them God's way.

The Big Idea

Stage 5 - Battle:

Conquering Your Circumstances

Trouble is normal and to be expected, but so is victory.

1. When trouble hits, find out what the Word says about your trouble.
2. Ask God what He wants you to do, and then do it.
3. Trust your faith instead of your feelings.

Notes

Stage 5 - Battle: Conquering Your Circumstances

Stage 6
Faith: The Battle for Success

This chapter is about the battle between doubt and faith.

In the last chapter we dealt with a tactical and biblical approach to conquering our circumstances. It is important to know, however, that biblical promises are gained by faith, not doubt. We must believe.

In this battle, there are two paths:

1. **Faith Leads to Success:** Faith > Expectation > Peace > Desire > Perseverance > Success

2. **Doubt Leads to Failure:** Doubt > Fear > Worry > Discouragement > Depression > Failure

Simply put … you become what you focus on.

Anytime we go to God in prayer, making requests based on His promises in the Word, asking for His help in some circumstance or situation, trust me; there will be a battle between doubt and faith. And there is rarely a victory without a battle.

SITUATION – You've lost your job and your resources are running low. You've gone to God for help.

First you see what the Word says about your situation. The battle begins.

You believe God will answer your prayers, and you are trusting Him for the how and the when. You are praising Him out of expectation. You are bold. You are confident. No weapon formed against you shall prosper. All things are possible through Christ who strengthens us. The devil is defeated. HALLELUJAH!

Perhaps these are the promises you are standing on:

Luke 11:9 (NIV) – So I say to you: Ask and it will be given to you; seek and you will find; knock and the door will be opened to you.

John 15:7 (NIV) – If you remain in me and my words remain in you, ask whatever you wish, and it will be done for you.

Mark 11:24 (NIV) – Therefore I tell you, whatever you ask for in prayer, believe that you have received it, and it will be yours.

Philippians 4:19 (NIV) – And my God will meet all your needs according to the riches of his glory in Christ Jesus.

Matthew 6:25-34 (NIV) – "Therefore I tell you, do not worry about your life, what you will eat or drink; or about your body, what you will wear. Is not life more than food, and the body more than clothes? Look at the birds of the air; they do not sow or reap or store away in barns, and yet your heavenly Father feeds them. Are you not much more valuable than they? Can any one of you by worrying add a single hour to your life?

"And why do you worry about clothes? See how the flowers of the field grow. They do not labor or spin. Yet I tell you that not even Solomon in all his splendor was dressed like one of these. If that is how God clothes the grass of the field, which is here today and tomorrow is thrown into the fire, will he not much more clothe you—you of little faith? So do not worry, saying, 'What shall we eat?' or 'What shall we drink?' or 'What shall we wear?' For the pagans run after all these things, and your heavenly Father knows that you need them. But seek first his kingdom and his righteousness, and all these things will be given to you as well. Therefore do not worry about tomorrow, for tomorrow will worry about itself. Each day has enough trouble of its own."

Matthew 7:9-11 (NIV) – "Which of you, if your son asks for bread, will give him a stone? Or if he asks for a fish, will give him a snake? If you, then, though you are evil, know how to give good gifts to your children, how much more will your Father in heaven give good gifts to those who ask him!"

FAITH VS. DOUBT

Then a doubt enters your thinking. Doubt is the opposite of faith. It is a thought contrary to your success. A thought contrary to the Word. A thought contrary to God's promises. The big question is, will you entertain the thought that does not line up with His Word and promises for you, or will you immediately rebuke this doubt as not from God?

The way to rebuke doubt is to first acknowledge the origin of the thought. When the doubt first enters my mind, I'll think or say, "That's not my thought. That's not God's thought. That thought came from the devil and I rebuke it in Jesus' name." Then I'll do as Jesus did in Matthew 4 when the devil tested Him – I'll respond with scripture. And if that thought keeps coming back, I'll demolish it with <u>lots</u> of scripture. As I find these scriptures, I'll write them down on index cards and carry them with me in my briefcase. I can't tell you how many times I couldn't sleep because I've woken up with thoughts of doubt. I've learned to get up, get my Word out, and start kicking the devil's rear end with it.

I've also learned not to wait until fighting time to begin my spiritual pushups because by then it's too late; the devil will have his way with me. When it comes to fighting time, you'd better have a few moves worked out in advance. We don't fight with will power; we fight with Word power. Never try to reason with the devil; He's mastered his game and will have you in doubt, fear, worry, discouragement, depression, and right to failure in the blink of an eye. Rebuke the thought and cast your cares over to Jesus.

2 Corinthians 10:5 (NIV) – We demolish arguments and every pretension that sets itself up against the knowledge of God, and we take captive every thought to make it obedient to Christ.

James 4:7 (NIV) – Submit yourselves, then, to God. Resist the devil, and he will flee from you.

Psalm 55:22 (NIV) – Cast your cares on the Lord and he will sustain you; he will never let the righteous be shaken.

1 Peter 5:7 (NIV) – Cast all your anxiety on him because he cares for you.

Or, you can choose not to.

Instead of focusing on the size of our God and the certainty of His promises, perhaps you allow yourself to focus on the size of your problem, knowing and admitting that while our almighty God CAN help you, you start to wonder if He really WILL. You begin to entertain the possibility that despite His many, many promises, maybe God won't come through for you. This is doubt.

Doubt seems like an innocent thought at first. After all, shouldn't you consider all the possibilities? So that's exactly what you begin to do, consider every NEGATIVE possibility. Then Satan begins to accuse you; he brings up your sin. His lies begin. His condemnation begins. If you choose to entertain doubt, just know that it ALWAYS progresses into fear. To stop doubt dead in its tracks, it must be immediately rebuked.

EXPECTATION VS. FEAR

If you rebuke doubt, your faith will progress to expectation. This is where you expect God to make good on His promises despite your present circumstances.

REMEMBER THE TWO PATHS:

Faith Leads to Success: Faith > Expectation > Peace > Desire > Perseverance > Success

Doubt Leads to Failure: Doubt > Fear > Worry > Discouragement > Depression > Failure

Hebrews 11:1 – (AMP) Now faith is the assurance (the confirmation, the title deed) of the things [we] hope for, being the proof of things [we] do not see *and* the conviction of their reality [faith perceiving as real fact what is not revealed to the senses].

I can remember when I was a growing up and "The Exorcist" was released in the movie theaters. It was about a young girl possessed by Satan. Everyone was talking about the movie, especially the scene where her head made a complete 360-degree turn. Very spooky. The rumor was that anyone who watched the movie could become possessed by Satan. That alone raised the curiosity of my friends and myself, not that we wanted to be possessed; we were just looking for a cheap thrill. My mom (aka "the church lady") forbid any of us to see this work of the devil. So naturally, we went to see the movie and it scared the wits out of us. None of us slept well for weeks. We couldn't get the scary images out of our minds. I should have listened to Mom! This is what fear does; it creates an image so scary that you end up frozen.

Fear is like making a movie called "The Downfall of You." Satan, the father of lies, presents you with the script; you produce it, direct it, and play the lead role. You take that unrebuked doubt and create a horror flick about your sorry situation. You conjure up the worst possible scene, thinking about all the terrible things that might happen to you. And then you somehow justify this thinking as "responsible thinking." Instead of meditating on God's Word, you choose to mediate on Satan's lies.

So you produce this worst-case scenario called fear, and then you begin to think about it over and over. You actually have a dress rehearsal in your mind; it's like allowing a child to watch "The Exorcist" over and over. That child is going to have some issues, or at the very least, messy pants.

Fear is an acronym for:

F-alse

E-vidence

A-ppearing

R-eal

Guess what? Your doubt grew into fear and now your fear just grew into full-blown worry. You can choose to rebuke this doubt and fear anytime; if you don't, see you on Worry Avenue.

PEACE VS. WORRY

THE TWO PATHS:

Faith Leads to Success: Faith > Expectation > Peace > Desire > Perseverance > Success

Doubt Leads to Failure: Doubt > Fear > Worry > Discouragement > Depression > Failure

The person who chooses faith and expectation gets peace. The person who allows fear begins to worry and is without peace.

Philippians 4:4-9 (MSG) – Celebrate God all day, every day. I mean, *revel* in him! Make it as clear as you can to all you meet that you're on their side, working with them and not against them. Help them see that the Master is about to arrive. He could show up any minute! Don't fret or worry. Instead of worrying, pray. Let petitions and praises shape your worries into prayers, letting God know your concerns. Before you know it, a sense of God's wholeness, everything coming together for good, will come and settle you down. It's wonderful what happens when Christ displaces worry at the center of your life. Summing it all up, friends, I'd say you'll do best by filling your minds and meditating on things true, noble, reputable, authentic, compelling, gracious—the best, not the worst; the beautiful, not the ugly; things to praise, not things to curse. Put into practice what you learned from me, what you heard and saw and realized. Do that, and God, who makes everything work together, will work you into his most excellent harmonies.

So what are we so worried about? I believe the following are the top two worries for us as Christians:

1. "Will God actually help me in this specific situation?"
2. "What will I have to go through before He does help me?"

Let's start with worrying if God will help you in this specific situation.

After you've spent time in the Word to see what God says about your situation, you have to decide if you really believe the Word. Most Christians believe that God CAN DO anything, but many are not quite sure what He WILL DO. And there's a huge gap between these two camps. It's hard to have faith in a God who *might* help you rather than a God you know *will* help you ... **with your specific situation.**

Never just settle for the opinions of other people. There is only one Bible, yet there are more than 41,000 Christian denominations in the world. That's at least 41,000 different opinions. So it's usually pretty easy to find someone to validate a truth or a lie. When in doubt, take it directly to God, and trust Him to show you the truth. That's why we have the Holy Spirit in us, to teach us and to comfort us. Understanding the path of truth will always require faith.

To have faith, you must know what you believe. Following are 31 logic points in understanding God's will. Each one builds upon the next. Go through them and decide what you believe. If you get stuck on one, take it to God. The Holy Spirit will lead you to the truth.

1. God is our Creator.

2. The Bible is God's Word.

3. The Word is His will.

4. God's will won't conflict with His Word.

5. What's possible can't be limited to what you presently know or believe.

6. When you are unsure, take it to God.

7. When you pray for God to help you, you must be specific and stand on God's Word.

8. You cannot be successful in fulfilling God's purpose if you don't know how to pray according to Biblical principles.

9. Your prayer life must be based upon the Word of God.

10. Faith begins where the Word of God (in context) is known.

11. If God's Word doesn't promise the things you are praying for, you shouldn't ask God for them.

12. You shouldn't want anything the Word says you shouldn't have.

13. If whatever you're praying for is in the Word, then it is the will of God.

14. When you get the Word firmly fixed in your heart and mind, then you can stand on (have faith and believe) it.

15. If God's Word states that something belongs to you, then it belongs to you.

16. If God didn't intend you to have what He promised you, then He wouldn't have promised it to you.

17. In order to fight the fight of faith, you must learn how to use the Word of God.

18. You must ask God for the things you want.

19. God knows what you need before you ask, but He still requires you to ask Him to help.

20. God doesn't force His help on you; if He did, then everyone would be saved and there would be no need or lack in this world.

21. You are to believe that you receive, right when you pray, despite your circumstances appearing unchanged.

22. In faith, you must believe you have your answer before you get it.

23. God provides everything you need in the spiritual realm of His Word.

24. When your circumstances conflict with God's promises, then you walk by what God states in His Word despite your circumstances.

25. By your faith you must accept ALL God's promises, and by your faith God makes good on ALL His promises.

26. Let every thought and desire affirm that you have what you ask for.

27. NEVER permit a mental picture of failure to remain in your mind.

28. If doubt persists, rebuke it.

29. Doubt is from the devil.

30. Fear is having more faith in the devil than in God's promises.

31. Reject EVERY thought that contradicts God's promises.

You see, most people believe *in* God. Even Satan believes in God. But not everyone actually *believes* God.

If you haven't invested time developing a two-way relationship with God in the Word, it's difficult to know what He'll actually do for you. You see, one can know a lot about someone without ever knowing him. This goes back to Stage 2, Hearing From God. It's hard to have a clear picture of who God is and what He's already done for you through the Word, Jesus Christ, and the Holy Spirit, without investing your time developing a two-way relationship with Him.

I often hear people pray, "If it's your will, Lord" or "God willing," and that's fine when we are seeking God's will and want to be in His will in making decisions. For instance, let's say you are offered a job in another city and you go to God for direction. That's exactly what you need to do because you won't find a scripture specifically telling you to move to San Antonio. But when the Word makes something abundantly clear, we don't have to keep asking God about His will – the Word is His will. If I seem to be struggling with doubt, fear, and worry, for instance, the Word makes it clear that I shouldn't. The phrase "Fear not" is in the Bible repeatedly. That should settle God's will for me on the matter. God promises to answer prayer. When God makes a promise, that's His will. And then it's my choice whether to believe it or not.

OK, so once you settle once and for all that you actually believe God and trust Him for the final outcome in your situation, you can address the second worry. Can you trust Him for the HOW and the WHEN? You see, somewhere between God's promise and the payoff is a process. Can you trust God to do what's best for you during the process? Let's examine the second worry.

The worry of what I'll have to go through before God answers my prayer.

Let's go back to the job-loss situation. Let's say you know that God's will is ultimately to answer your prayer. Now Satan will come along with another set of doubt, fear, and worry. You'll have thoughts such as:

Well, I'm almost out of money; how am I going to pay rent?
God's going to allow me to lose everything to humble me.

If you entertain these thoughts, you'll start to have doubt, fear, and worry about what God will allow you to go through. This is where you must trust God to do what's best for you and trust Him with the how and the when. Again, instead of focusing on all the "what ifs," focus on God's promises in His Word.

If you allow yourself to worry, it will quickly progress to discouragement.

DESIRE VS. DISCOURAGEMENT

THE TWO PATHS:

Faith Leads to Success: Faith > Expectation > Peace > Desire > Perseverance > Success

Doubt Leads to Failure: Doubt > Fear > Worry > Discouragement > Depression > Failure

So, you have a choice; you can see what the Word says about your situation in this order:

1. **Read** the Word.
2. **Believe** the Word.
3. **Receive** the Word by faith.
4. **Speak** the Word.
5. **Do** what the Word says.

If you do these things, you will have faith, expectation, peace (zero worry or concern), and a desire to walk with confidence on your journey. If you don't, you will eventually become discouraged. Discouragement is walking your journey without courage. People become discouraged when they lose hope. People often tell me, "But Gerald, everyone gets discouraged." Not so. At times everyone becomes momentarily disappointed, but our faith refreshes us through the tough times. We may get tired, but we don't have to become discouraged.

Discouragement is walking without confidence in God. You see, our confidence is in Jesus, not ourselves. Our faith is in Jesus. The Bible instructs us to be encouraged, never discouraged. We are instructed to have courage. This is faith. Realize that your feelings and your faith are not the same. Faith is a belief. Feelings are emotions.

> Joshua 1:5-7 (NIV) – No one will be able to stand against you all the days of your life. As I was with Moses, so I will be with you; I will never leave you nor forsake you. Be strong and courageous, because you will lead these people to inherit the land I swore to their ancestors to give them. "Be strong and very courageous. Be careful to obey all the law my servant Moses gave you; do not turn from it to the right or to the left, that you may be successful wherever you go."

> Deuteronomy 31:6 (NIV) – "Be strong and courageous. Do not be afraid or terrified because of them, for the Lord your God goes with you; he will never leave you nor forsake you."

When we become discouraged, we lose our courage to move forward. The last thing we want to do is get stuck in the desert. You see, life is full of peaks and valleys. And there is not much learning happening on the mountaintops. The mountaintops are where we celebrate. The bulk of our learning occurs in the valleys of life. This is where our faith gets tested, where we learn patience and perseverance.

Somewhere in your life journey, you'll get a flat tire in the desert. For a time, you get stuck there. It's dry in the desert season, not a whole lot of provision there. You might have to camp out there for just a little while, but don't build your house there; remember that you're just passing through. Praise God for that!

People who become discouraged lose sight of their destination; they are often confused by life's path, and sometimes they lose all hope.

Eventually, they get bitter, not better. They become victims of their circumstances. If that's you, you must choose faith to get out. Find out what the Word says about your situation. Choose faith and start walking toward your destiny. God will be with you every step of the way. And before you know it, you'll get your expectation back, then your peace, and finally your desire to trust God.

The sad news is discouraged people eventually become depressed people. Remember, the choice is yours.

PERSEVERANCE VS. DEPRESSION

THE TWO PATHS:

Faith Leads to Success: Faith > Expectation > Peace > Desire > Perseverance > Success

Doubt Leads to Failure: Doubt > Fear > Worry > Discouragement > Depression > Failure

The truth is, there are people prone to depression. Their feelings are powerful and their fight of faith might be greater than yours or mine. Yet, through Christ, they can persevere. You see, the Word doesn't work only for those who are not prone to depression. It works for all. The Word conquers all.

Wrong thinking leads to lasting depression. It's times like these we need to ask God for an aerial view. Ask God to allow us to see our situation from His view. A Word view. One thing I can say with complete confidence is that God is NEVER depressed. You'd think our creator would get depressed with His creation more than anyone since His view includes all of man's atrocities and sins. But you see, God has a plan, a plan for the universe, and a plan for each one of us. A plan to prosper us. How do I know that? The Bible says so and that settles it for me.

Sometimes when you are stuck in the desert, it's hard to see around the corner.

In 2007, my precious son Alec got sick and was admitted to the hospital. Because he had Down Syndrome, he had gone through many open-heart surgeries. But at ten years old, he was really healthy considering all he had been through. We had just been in to see the cardiologist for his annual checkup and he was doing great. But we were familiar with the hospital drill; we never knew if we were coming home anytime soon. This time, he kept getting sicker and sicker, and no one could figure out what was wrong. During a routine kidney biopsy to figure out what was wrong, he went into cardiac arrest and died on the operating table. No parent should have to experience the sight of his or her child dead. For us, this was a desert season.

In our grieving, we had a battle on our hands. A faith battle. How could God let this happen? We asked God to give us an aerial view, to allow us to see things from His perspective. He did. God allowed us the perspective of knowing that Alec is more alive in heaven today than he ever was on earth, that he is completely healed, something we prayed for every day of his life. And when Leslie and I have fulfilled God's plan and purpose for us here on earth, we will get to be with him in heaven. He'd be waiting for us. The knowledge that Alec was completely fulfilled in heaven, and didn't want to come back gave us so much comfort and peace. Wow! What an awesome perspective that dulled the sting of his departure from earth.

I knew I couldn't allow wrong thinking about my son's death to set my focus. The devil did his best to tempt me to take my focus off God's Word and place it onto my circumstances. Sometime later we learned Alec's death was due to a heart medicine overdose, caused by a pharmaceutical manufacturing mistake. But none of this changed the outcome;

my son was now living with Jesus. I wasn't about to let anger, blame, or hate to get into my spirit. How did we overcome this and not get depressed? We stayed glued to God's Word, trusting Him no matter what, praising Him no matter what. We got better, not bitter.

I don't know what horrifying circumstances you are experiencing today. What I do know is that your situation hasn't taken God by surprise. God's not wringing His hands, wondering what's He's going to do. Our God has a plan to help you and to prosper you through your situation. Trust me; ongoing depression is not part of His plan for you.

What we learn through our tough times is patience and perseverance.

James 1:2-4 (NIV) – Consider it pure joy, my brothers and sisters, whenever you face trials of many kinds, because you know that the testing of your faith produces perseverance. Let perseverance finish its work so that you may be mature and complete, not lacking anything.

Hebrews 6:11-12 – (KJV) And we desire that every one of you do shew the same diligence to the full assurance of hope unto the end: That ye be not slothful, but followers of them who through faith and patience inherit the promises.

Perseverance is never quitting, no matter what. When you get to the end of your rope, tie a knot and hold on. If you are prone to depression, never quit your battle; God is with you and His grace is enough to carry you through the tough times.

2 Corinthians 12:9 (NIV) – But he said to me, "My grace is sufficient for you, for my power is made perfect in weakness." Therefore I will boast all the more gladly about my weaknesses, so that Christ's power may rest on me.

SUCCESS VS. FAILURE

THE TWO PATHS:

Faith Leads to Success: Faith > Expectation > Peace > Desire > Perseverance > Success

Doubt Leads to Failure: Doubt > Fear > Worry > Discouragement > Depression > Failure

Success is simply a choice to allow God to build your faith by developing a two-way relationship with Him. A faith relationship. On the other hand, doubt is a wild seed. If you allow doubt to get planted in your mind, YOU WILL FAIL. If doubt is not dealt with quickly, it grows into fear, then worry, then discouragement, then depression, and then failure.

We must become spiritual optimists during our fight of faith. We all know life is full of peaks and valleys. While God is not the author of valleys or tough times, if we allow Him, He promises to help us climb out. Valleys are the work of the devil even when self-inflicted. As we gain Godly wisdom, knowledge, and understanding, we will develop the ability to spot many valleys in advance and simply soar over them. We do not have to descend into every valley, but if we do, God will be with us.

Did you know our perception of the valleys we go through frames our future? We rarely appreciate the valleys while we are in them, but we become thankful when we reach the mountaintop because of what God has taught us. Oftentimes it's the valleys that allow us to see and truly appreciate His grace and mercy on us. God's mercy is not getting what we deserve, and God's grace is <u>getting what we don't deserve</u>. And be assured, we will experience both as we climb out of our lows.

Our perception of God, His promises, our circumstances, and ourselves will always shape our belief of what is possible. Our belief of what's possible will always shape our goals, our goals will shape our choices and decisions, and our decisions will inevitably shape our results.

PERCEPTION > BELIEF > GOALS > DECISIONS > RESULTS

We can see that our perception determines our results, but what determines our perception? Our perception is determined by the condition of our hearts, and the condition of our hearts is determined by what we invite, allow, or put in our minds.

Again, if we allow doubt in, doubt leads to fear, fear leads to worry, worry leads to discouragement, discouragement leads to depression, and depression leads to failure.

DOUBT > FEAR > WORRY > DISCOURAGEMENT > DEPRESSION > FAILURE

But when we know what God's plan and purpose for our life is, that we have a destination, we know where we're going. We have vision. And when we have vision, we hope for the future. When we don't have a destination, it's easy to doubt where we're going. Can you start to see why knowing God's plan and purpose for your life is critical for Christian success?

So let's identify your current attitude. Are you in doubt, fear, worry, discouragement, or depression? Now look up every scripture you can find on doubt, fear, worry, discouragement, or depression and see what God says about it. Now look up faith and you will learn how to get it.

You don't get faith because you are strong or because you have a lot of will power. Faith comes by hearing the Word of God. When you get into the Word and God's promises become your focus, you become what you focus on. Your faith increases, you expect to succeed, you have God's perfect peace (while you're in the valley), you have joy, your desire to continue your journey is ignited, and you develop perseverance. And before you know it, you're on the mountaintop.

You've heard "Attitude is everything." Well, it's true: your perspective will determine your results. Fear tolerated is faith contaminated. You must guard your mind. Your faith attitude determines your altitude.

FEAR NOT and HAVE FAITH. These four words must become our default response to every circumstance. Are you a spiritual optimist or pessimist? A spiritual pessimist will win few faith battles.

The Big Idea

Stage 6 - Faith: The Battle for Success

The battle for success or failure takes place in the your mind. It is in our minds where we decide what we will allow to win in our life, doubt or faith. Who we will believe, God or Satan?

1. Faith Leads to Success: Faith > Expectation > Peace > Desire > Perseverance > Success

2. Doubt Leads to Failure: Doubt > Fear > Worry > Discouragement > Depression > Failure

Notes

Stage 7

Purpose: Identifying God's Plan for You

C ongratulations! You've made it to Stage 7 where you can now learn how to identify God's plan and purpose for your life. What we are after is a vision from God and then some first steps. First, you need the vision from God. You may ask, "Gerald, will I have a dream, see writing on the wall, see an actual vision, or get to watch a bush burn like Moses did?" Well maybe, but probably not. God will begin to unveil His planted purpose that He has already planted deep inside you. You might already have an idea of what your calling is, but perhaps you lack clarity or the first steps ordained by God Himself. There are only two simple, and yet complex, steps involved in getting this incredible vision that is sure to give birth to a whole new chapter in your life. Before you take the first steps of God's plan and purpose for your life, be sure you already have these foundational steps under your belt:

1. Receive the full knowledge (of the actual existence) of a plan and purpose for your life.

2. Begin seeking God with this knowledge to connect with His plan for your life.

Keep in mind that God's number one plan and purpose for your life will always be your relationship and fellowship with Him. This must be number one for you. This means you are willing to put your life in His hands and then trust Him completely with it, no matter what!

The projects or assignments He gives you will always be secondary in importance to your relationship with Him. To have this relationship with Him, one where you trust Him completely, you'll need to have already taken the following growth steps covered in Stages 1 through 6:

1. You believe and receive the inheritance the blood of Jesus bought at the cross and through the resurrection. – HPMP Stage 1

2. As a result of much time invested in the Word and prayer, you have a two-way relationship with God. – HPMP Stage 2

3. You have given God permission to change your way of thinking to His way of thinking. – HPMP Stage 3

4. As a result of changing your way of thinking to His way, you've also changed your way of doing to His way. – HPMP Stage 4

5. You know how to effectively put on the armor of Christ, allowing God to conquer your circumstances for you through His Word. – HPMP Stage 5

6. You walk by faith, not by doubt. – HPMP Stage 6

I call these stages "the basics," of your foundation. Without the foundation, your house will crumble under pressure from life's storms.

Doubt, fear, and worry will stop you dead in your tracks. You might be born again and saved, but you'll always be living beneath your privilege. So check these foundational stages and see if you have given God control of each area of your life. Trusting God completely is the prerequisite to identifying and beginning to fulfill His plan and purpose for your life. It also makes your relationship with Him your number one priority.

There are two types of Christians on earth, those who know why God put them on the planet, and those who don't. The fact is, God has a master plan, and you are part of it. The question is do you have a desire to know it and do it? Most Christians agree that God has a plan and purpose for their lives, but for whatever reason, even as Christians, they seem to be completely fine with not knowing what it is.

This is Satan's gigantic deception. In fact, while the church believes God has a plan and purpose for you, hardly anyone asks why so few seem to know what it is. How strange!

Think about it. Like the message of the Gospel, outside of our comfortable church circles, we barely mention it. Go figure. As I said previously, recent church research indicates that less than 1 percent of churches are successfully reaching the unchurched. Even stranger. The fact is, when the body of Christ, the church, does not know its individual and corporate purpose, it becomes dysfunctional.

I mean really, if you had the cure for cancer, and people all around you had cancer, wouldn't you be talking about it? It's with that same passion that I want to help you identify and fulfill God's plan and purpose for your life.

God's plan and purpose for you will blow the socks off anything you could come up with on your own. Nothing in life can or will even come close. You already have special God-given gifts inside you that are unique to your purpose. Why? Because deep inside you is a God-planted purpose.

Get ready; God is about to unearth this dream inside you, expose it, and grow it into its full destiny.

Ephesians 2:10 (AMP) – For we are God's [own] handiwork (His workmanship), recreated in Christ Jesus, [born anew] that we may do those good works which God predestined (planned beforehand) for us [taking paths which He prepared ahead of time], that we should walk in them [living the good life which He prearranged and made ready for us to live].

You were created to do more than you are presently doing. The reason you are frustrated is because you don't know what you were created to do. This is why you are reading this book. So where do you start? Let's begin with step one.

Step One – Knowledge

The journey begins with gaining knowledge. Without knowledge, "God's know-how," we'll never progress far in our purpose.

Hosea 4:6 (NIV) – my people are destroyed from lack of knowledge...

James 1:5 (NIV) – If any of you lacks wisdom, you should ask God, who gives generously to all without finding fault, and it will be given to you.

Matthew 19:26 – (KJV) But Jesus beheld them, and said unto them, With men this is impossible; but with God all things are possible.

The first step in identifying God's plan and purpose for your life is getting the knowledge of these three truths inside you. They must become part of your personal belief and spiritual knowledge. You must let God convert the intellectual information that resides in your brain to heart-felt knowledge and truth that resides in your heart.

Truth #1 – God has a master plan and purpose for your life.

Jeremiah 1:5 (NIV) – "Before I formed you in the womb I knew you, before you were born I set you apart; I appointed you as a prophet to the nations."

Jeremiah 29:11 (NIV) – "For I know the plans I have for you," declares the Lord, "plans to prosper you and not to harm you, plans to give you hope and a future."

Ephesians 1:4-5; 11 (NIV) – For he chose us in him before the creation of the world to be holy and blameless in his sight. In love he predestined us for adoption to sonship through Jesus Christ, in accordance with his pleasure and will—vs. 11 In him we were also chosen, having been predestined according to the plan of him who works out everything in conformity with the purpose of his will,

Truth #2 – God will reveal His plan (for you) to you.

Psalm 16:11 (NIV) – You make known to me the path of life; you will fill me with joy in your presence, with eternal pleasures at your right hand.

Ephesians 1:9 (NIV) – he made known to us the mystery of his will according to his good pleasure, which he purposed in Christ,

Ephesians 1:17-18 (NIV) – I keep asking that the God of our Lord Jesus Christ, the glorious Father, may give you the Spirit of wisdom and revelation, so that you may know him better. I pray that the eyes of your heart may be enlightened in order that you may know the hope to which he has called you, the riches of his glorious inheritance in his holy people,

Colossians 1:9 (NIV) – For this reason, since the day we heard about you, we have not stopped praying for you. We continually ask God to fill you with the knowledge of his will through all the wisdom and understanding that the Spirit gives,

James 1:5 (NIV) – If any of you lacks wisdom, you should ask God, who gives generously to all without finding fault, and it will be given to you.

Truth #3 – No person or thing can stop His plan for you … Except You!

Psalm 138:8 (NIV) – The Lord will vindicate me; your love, Lord, endures forever— do not abandon the works of your hands.

Philippians 1:6 (NIV) – being confident of this, that he who began a good work in you will carry it on to completion until the day of Christ Jesus.

Job 42:2 (NIV) – "I know that you can do all things; no purpose of yours can be thwarted."

Psalm 33:11 (NIV) – But the plans of the Lord stand firm forever, the purposes of his heart through all generations.

Romans 8:28 (NIV) – And we know that in all things God works for the good of those who love him, who have been called according to his purpose.

While most people have heard and agree with the idea that God has a plan and purpose for their lives, it is not something they can actually prove with scripture. When the Holy Spirit reveals a biblical truth to you, it becomes a revelation to you. It goes into your heart and begins to come out of your mouth. The knowledge becomes part of you. This is where information transforms into knowledge that you'll base your faith on. This is sometimes referred to as revelation knowledge. Revelation knowledge comes through investing time meditating on God's Word.

Set some time aside to search out scriptures that answer the following three questions:

1. How do you know that God has a plan and purpose for your life?
2. How can you be confident that if you seek out God, you'll find what you are looking for?
3. How can you be sure that even if you come to understand God's plan and purpose for your life, that you can successfully fulfill it?

Take a few weeks to search out God's Word, and spend some serious time with God in prayer. You may even consider fasting during part of this time. You'll come to a place where you become absolutely confident that God really has a plan and purpose for your life.

For too many Christians this is only intellectual information. And while they may agree that God has a plan and a purpose for everyone, **they've allowed Satan to reduce their idea of what that plan actually is … to what they are already doing.** A mother might rationalize, for example, "God's plan for me is to be a good mother to my children." Well of course God wants you to be a good parent. God wanted Abraham to be a good parent. But there was more to God's plan for Abraham than that. God also wanted Jesus to be a good son to Joseph and Mary, but as we know, there was more to God's plan than that. And that doesn't in any way minimize the importance of being a great mother or son, but there is always more to God's plans than just being good in your current role in life. Don't take the easy way out; get out of your comfort zone, which will take you to step two.

Step Two – Seek out God

If you want to connect with God's master plan and purpose for your life, you must search out God's truths for your life. This only happens when, because of your relationship with God, you make a quality choice to really get to know Him by walking in fellowship with Him. As you begin to walk in this fellowship with God, tell Him that you know that you know … that you know … that you know that He has a plan and purpose for your life, and that you are seeking to learn what it is. Begin to thank Him in advance for the upcoming revelation and journey that lies ahead. Ask God to prepare your heart and to reveal anything in your life that is not pleasing to Him so that with His help, you can be set free from whatever hinders you.

The Big Idea

Stage 7 - Faith:
Identifying God's Plan for You

As you gain the revelation knowledge that God actually has a very specific plan and purpose for your life (when you know that you know that you know), you'll develop an insatiable desire to identify what it is. This desire will launch you into a season of seeking, dreaming, and exploring what God Himself wants for your life, followed by a response from you to dedicate your whole life to His service. I call this on-boarding.

1. Develop the revelation knowledge and desire to know what His plan for you is.
2. Seek, seek, seek, and keep seeking.
3. Give yourself completely to God. Everything!

Notes

Stage 7 - Faith: Identifying God's Plan for You

Stage 8

Start: Taking Your First Step

A s God begins to speak His vision into you, you will have to receive it by faith because it will be bigger than anything you could ever accomplish alone.

That said, ponder for a moment why faith is such a mandatory factor in obeying God's vision for your life. Aside from the fact that we can't please God without faith, we also can't fathom the path that will lead to our destiny without the faith to call what is not as though it were.

Hebrews 11:1 (NIV) – Now faith is confidence in what we hope for and assurance about what we do not see.

Without faith, our minds just can't map it, as there will be plenty of unanswered questions and impossibilities to work through as we follow the path God lays out for us. The vision is often blurry as a result of self-perpetuating negative filters, which if allowed, will cause our perception of God to be smaller than the mountains we face, and we will actually distort what's possible through Christ. Many of us have spent years erecting and allowing invisible boundaries designed to keep us in our place. And while we might be eagles designed to soar, regrettably, we're living like chickens in a chicken coop.

If our connection to God is not secured through relationship and fellowship with Him, our thoughts will be cluttered with the static of our past limited experiences. Like a monitor to a computer, we must stay firmly connected to our source to maintain a clear picture. Without faith, we'll most likely miss the onramp to our journey and possibly the first step to our destiny. We need to be firmly connected to God and His plan and purpose for our lives.

So how does God begin to reveal His plan and purpose to us?

1. His methods for revealing His plan to us can vary drastically.

    You may have an idea or a desire that just won't go away, perhaps something that has always been on your heart but it never seemed feasible. Maybe you've been waiting for your ship to come in not realizing you are actually the ship. Sometimes when we are too "realistic," we don't leave room for the super- natural. When people say "I'm just being realistic" or "just being real," that's generally code for one's inability to think past their circumstances. It's a very common excuse. Happens more often than naught. Why would anyone limit what's possible to their past limited experiences? You'll find that God expects to put some of His SUPER on your NATURAL.

2. Don't expect to receive or know every detail.

    What we'd all love to receive from God is a franchise kit, complete with detailed instructions, a journey map, supply inventory, and an operating manual. Our operating manual is called the Bible, and inside that manual are more than 6,000 promises to handle any and every circumstance we might encounter on our journey. But you can probably forget the franchise kit.

3. One of the hardest things to accept is that we are on a need-to-know basis with God.

    He tells us what we need to know when we need to know it. Sometimes we receive information years in advance, and other times we get it at the very last moment. Think of Joseph and his dream. He received some of his information years and years before it came true. The same is true of David and Abraham. But when the Israelites crossed the Red Sea, God didn't provide Moses with the instructions until the very last moment, when failure seemed certain. I'm sure the parting of the Red Sea was well beyond what anyone thought possible, despite the numerous miracles the Israelites had already witnessed.

4. Your gifts and talents are unique to your purpose and not by mistake.

    Some people's gifts and talents are really obvious like someone with a great singing voice. But others, like Moses, had gifts only God could see. They are like diamonds in the rough feeling underqualified for what God has called them to do. But whether their gifts are obvious or not, God custom fitted them for His plan and purpose for your life.

5. We can only see part of the journey.

    Which part? The part God wants you to see. So don't try to figure everything out in advance. When we do, we find ourselves forcing situations and seasons when we are simply not ready or adequately prepared to succeed. God's plan and purpose for your life is not a destination but a journey filled with rich fellowship with God Himself, and with various assignments, missions, and seasons.

    Learn to embrace and make the most of every step of the journey. The fire will purify you, and the tests will develop patience and perseverance, until ultimately, you'll become totally dependent on God for everything.

6. God's plan and purpose is not a destination; it's a journey.

    Have you watched a popular television series? It consists of seasons and episodes written by a team of writers. Similarly, God's plan and purpose for our lives is sort of like a reality show complete with seasons and episodes. God, the writer, producer, and director of our lives, is in complete control of every detail of our journey. So we must get comfortable with allowing Him to direct our every step.

Is the vision from God?

1. As God begins to share His vision with you, take your time praying about it.

    Let God prove to you that the vision is really from Him and not just something you conjured up in your mind. When it's God, you'll eventually have peace even when faced with a difficult or seemingly impossible assignment. Impossible is a flesh word. Nothing is impossible for God. Impossibilities are only the entrance to God's miracles.

2. Keep these dreams close to the vest.

Don't share them with everyone. Remember, Joseph ended up in a hole to die because he couldn't keep his mouth shut. In the beginning, share your dreams, but only with trusted advisors. God will bring people to help and encourage you along the way. Don't be surprised when friends and family attempt to discourage you from taking risks. Many times their focus is on you, your imperfections and lack of experience. What they fail to understand is when God calls man, who by the way was made after His very own image, He chooses them for their obedience, not their experience or ability. God's not concerned about our past; He's looking for those who will walk by faith, trusting Him for everything required.

1 Corinthians 1:27 (MSG) – Take a good look, friends, at who you were when you got called into this life. I don't see many of "the brightest and the best" among you, not many influential, not many from high-society families. Isn't it obvious that God deliberately chose men and women that the culture overlooks and exploits and abuses, chose these "nobodies" to expose the hollow pretensions of the "somebodies"? That makes it quite clear that none of you can get by with blowing your own horn before God. Everything that we have—right thinking and right living, a clean slate and a fresh start—comes from God by way of Jesus Christ. That's why we have the saying, "If you're going to blow a horn, blow a trumpet for God."

3. Don't assume every open or closed door (circumstance) is from God.

    Some people wrongly assume that every open or closed door is from God. Some are and some aren't. And when the door won't open or access appears blocked, like the walls of Jericho, people can mistake the shut doors as a NO from God. When mountains block our path, we sometimes mistakenly turn around and head the wrong way, assuming God shut the door.

    Mark 11:23 (NIV) – "Truly I tell you, if anyone says to this mountain, 'Go, throw yourself into the sea,' and does not doubt in their heart but believes that what they say will happen, it will be done for them."

That's why we need mountain-moving faith to allow God to open closed doors and remove the obstacles that block His path for us.

Throughout every journey, there are on-ramps and off-ramps. Think about a road trip you have taken. Usually we have some type of time-frame or schedule to keep. Even on leisurely trips, most of us wouldn't purposely stop somewhere and camp out for 20 years. We may stop to eat, refuel, or rest for a night or two, but then we get back on the highway and journey toward our destination. Along the way we'll see many road signs to destinations that may appear enticing, but if we take them, we can easily get sidetracked and never reach our destination.

Remember, Satan can open and close doors too! We can also wrongly force doors open or shut. This is why it is so important for us to always be connected to God. At times when you feel disconnected, STOP and take time to reconnect. Get alone with God and listen. He is our life GPS. If you get a little lost, reconnect.

4. You'll know it's from God if:

    a. It's impossible without a miracle.

    b. You can't let go of it.

    c. It builds and glorifies the Kingdom of God.

    d. You are willing to dedicate your whole life to it.

    e. You are willing to give up everything for it.

Getting started.

1. Write it down.

    When God begins to present you with a vision of a direction or destiny for your life, always write it down.

    Habakkuk 2:2 (MSG) – And then God answered: "Write this. Write what you see. Write it out in big block letters so that it can be read on the run. This vision-message is a witness pointing to what's coming. It aches for the coming—it can hardly wait! And it doesn't lie. If it seems slow in coming, wait. It's on its way. It will come right on time."

2. Commit to allowing God to prepare you for your purpose.

    Faith, obedience, love, forgiveness, humility, gratefulness, confidence, patience, perseverance, diligence, wisdom ... these are just some of the necessary characteristics required of you to fulfill God's plan and purpose for your life. We don't get all these things by sitting in a chair, reading books; going to church; or praying. We gain access to these character traits through experiences, failures, test, trials, and desert seasons. People who are strong in these areas have gone through some stuff. They've been through some valleys and have gotten dirty.

You don't get faith unless you've been through some doubt. You're not obedient unless you've allowed God to crucify some sin in your life. You don't learn to forgive unless someone has done you dirty. You don't find humility until you've been broken and put your pride to bed. You develop gratefulness by learning to go without. You develop confidence by trusting God through your failure. God has developed patience in you by allowing you to suffer through some desert seasons. You've gained perseverance by not giving in to the part of you that wants to give up when no hope is in sight. And you now have diligence and wisdom by making it through all the above. God develops all these character traits by testing and perfecting your faith. If you want to attend God's finishing school, you'll have to get in the fire. Do you trust God enough to take you through whatever is necessary to prepare you for His plan and purpose for your life? To prepare and teach you how to succeed God's way? This is the requirement. Period.

3. When you take the first step, wait for God's green light instead of what you perceive are ideal conditions.

   Is God waiting on us or are we waiting on God? In the past when God has shown me a vision of what He wants done, I've mistaken that for the green light and experienced unfortunate false starts, meaning I've tried to force things to happen. Trust me; this never ends well and it's extremely frustrating. So when God reveals something to me, my flesh nature tries to figure out everything for myself. I attempt to create a path I think is the shortest distance from point A to point B, an easy straight line.

But once you've been around God's plans for a while, you learn that few paths seem direct or straight in the beginning. The journey is usually on a winding road that God will eventually make straight. Getting started usually means taking some first steps that really don't make sense. And yet God asks for our obedience to trust in Him. Much of the time God is waiting for us to take that first step in faith.

John 10:4 (AMP) – When he has brought his own sheep outside, he walks on before them, and the sheep follow him because they know his voice.

This is why having two-way communication with God is vital. Even when we get it wrong, we can always go back to God, ask Him what went wrong, and learn from our mistakes. He will always get us back on track; it's never too late.

4. Getting started.

As God lays out His vision to you, your first step is to receive it by faith. This means realizing the assignment isn't some great thing you have to do with God's help. **It's an act of God that He's allowed you to participate in.** All He wants you to do is accept the mission.

After you've accepted the mission, seek God to reveal the what, the how, and the why of the assignment. This is a great time to fast. Acknowledge the size of the mission, understanding that you are not capable of accomplishing it alone. Then acknowledge the size of your God, understanding that God is able to accomplish it (without your help). You should be having a lot of "God, I don't know how" and "God, will you show me?" conversations with Him.

Then make a commitment to a faith journey, understanding the battle is not yours, but God's. Allow Him to fight your battles. Once you accept the assignment, by faith begin praising God in advance of every victory, remembering that if this assignment is from Him, you might stumble, you might be delayed, but you will never be denied because God never fails ... ever!

The Big Idea

Stage 8 - Start: Taking Your First Step

Before you start, STOP. Make sure God has ordained each step that you take. By doing so, you'll avoid some painful false starts. Allow God to prepare you for each step before you take it. Don't fight or skip the preparation. Without it you will fail.

1. Stop.
2. Listen.
3. Learn.

Notes

Stage 8 - Start: Taking Your First Step

Stage 9

Provision: God is Our Source

God is our provider.

God is generous and it is His will to give us all of Himself. This includes material provision. As you read through the Bible, the message of God providing for us is inescapable. And more importantly, God wants us to trust Him for everything … both spiritual and material. If we do trust Him, He promises to provide. Again, God wants to be our source for everything. He is our provider. This is His will. Our will must be to trust God completely for all provision.

Matthew 6:33 (NIV) – But seek first his kingdom and his righteousness, and all these things will be given to you as well.

I love the way The Message Bible lays this out.

Matthew 6:33 (MSG) – If God gives such attention to the appearance of wildflowers—most of which are never even seen—don't you think he'll attend to you, take pride in you, do his best for you? What I'm trying to do here is to get you to relax, to not be so preoccupied with *getting*, so you can respond to God's *giving*. People who don't know God and the way he works fuss over these things, but you know both God and how he works. Steep your life in God-reality, God-initiative, God-provisions. Don't worry about missing out. You'll find all your everyday human concerns will be met."

You see, though God is our provider, He doesn't want us to be pre-occupied with "getting." We should focus on building our relationship with the giver instead of focusing on getting what we want when we want it. As a father I am the provider and the giver of gifts. I love giving to my children, but I want my children to love me for me, not for the gifts they may get from me. If I sensed they only wanted the gifts, the gifts would stop; the provision would not, though the level of provision might. They have to eat, right? But perhaps no steak tonight. This is about our atti-tude toward our relationship with God.

One thing is for sure: it's impossible to be in God's will and not re-ceive God's provision. God always provides, no matter what. But God's promises come with a big IF. If we do, He will provide. We must trust Him for His HOW and WHEN.

Temporary seasons of want or lack

If God is our provider, what about seasons of want or lack? Most of us will experience these seasons. And we can be walking right in His will when we do. This is when God doesn't give us ***what we want when we want*** *it* or when He <u>allows</u> ***what we have to be taken away*** from us. Though these seasons can be extremely painful and confusing, notice how you didn't die of starvation during the temporary season of lack. God still provides, just not to our level of want. He sometimes withholds material provision for a season to grow us so we can trust Him and so He can trust us with both blessings and trials.

God uses these seasons to draw us closer to Him and prepare our hearts for the great things He has for us. His will for us during these incredibly tough seasons is to stretch our trust and faith in Him. This is a painful process of very personal and spiritual growth. If we'll trust Him, we'll experience God's miracles. It is not possible for God to fail someone who puts his or her complete trust in Him. During these tough times, and despite our circumstances, we learn that God is in control and can make ANYTHING happen, especially when it defies all logic.

When God takes all you have from you, it's only to make room for Him to fill us with EVERYTHING He wants us to have. When He does this, He is dealing with our hearts. God builds a relationship with us first, and out of that will come His FULL PROVISION. There are about 6,000 promises in the Bible and God's Word is His will. It's His will to make good on every promise.

Don't forget about the "ifs." Some will manifest this side of Heaven; others will be on the other side. Remember, this part of our lives is very temporary and momentary compared to the eternal life we will have. Just remember, God is our provider. When it's His will, He pays the bill. We might have to march around Jericho a bunch of times, and He may ask you do something that seems illogical, but God is the one who directs our steps, so trust Him completely and step forward into your destiny.

The Big Idea

Stage 9 - Provision: God is Our Source

Who's your provider? Your employer? Your business? You? or God? This is something you'll have to settle in your heart. It's really your choice. Once it's settled, however, assuming you chose God, provision is a matter of faith. When the bills come in you can say, "Lord, you've got mail!"

1. Pick your provider.
2. Trust your provider.

Notes

Stage 9 - Provision: God is Our Source

Stage 10
Prosperity: The High-Faith Believer

Does God want us to prosper?

If you are looking for an opinion on what God says about prosperity, you can find one that will match whatever it is you want to believe. Christians tend to throw around the word *prosperity* like we do *progressive, liberal,* or *conservative* to place people at odds with our beliefs into camps. We don't like differences or disagreements. Having said all that, *prosperity,* for whatever reason, has become a bad word to many Christians. The problem is instead of defining what it actually means, we decide we just don't like it.

And we certainly don't like the prosperity preachers. That's a label we attach to those with whom we vehemently disagree and assign to the heretic camp, just like we do when we label someone *progressive, conservative, republican, democrat, socialist,* or worse, *a no-good communist.* Those who are banished to one of these camps are there for good.

Fact is, we use our words to judge, slander, and condemn those we disagree with, much of the time without a lot of thought. As a result, sadly, many have stopped asking God to prosper them, even though He makes it clear that He desires to prosper us. And whether or not we receive or reject His prosperity here on earth, when we get to heaven, even the stubborn will be prosperous. After all, it is God's will, so who are you to challenge God?

Before we get too far, let's address what Biblical prosperity is NOT:

- Prosperity is not a life without trouble.
- Prosperity is not a get-rich-quick scheme.
- Prosperity is not tricking God into giving you more.
- Prosperity isn't something God will grant you when your heart isn't right.
- Prosperity isn't something God will grant you if you are walking outside of His will.
- Prosperity isn't a luxury lifestyle.
- Prosperity isn't being rich as the world defines *rich*.

It's important to know that the words *prosper, prosperity, and prosperous* are in the Bible more than 80 times. If you search for the word *prosper* at www.biblegateway.com, you will get a list of each instance. Read these scriptures and you will have a hard time believing that God doesn't want you to prosper. To prosper is a good thing, not a bad thing.

Webster's definition: the condition of being successful or thriving; especially: economic well-being.

Hebrew definition 6743: tranquility; security, ease, peace, wealth, to have good success.

Greek definition 2137: to help on the road; succeed in reaching, to succeed in business affairs.

Prosper is a biblical word. So as you read the Bible, you'll get the impression that God wants you to be prosperous. Our approach on any topic should be to see what the Bible says. We should do our homework and allow the Holy Spirit to guide us. If you lived when Jesus walked the earth and you had a question about anything spiritual, whom would you ask, Jesus or His disciples? You would go to the source, right? You would ask Jesus Himself. Well, guess what? Nothing has changed.

"Well, Gerald, Jesus is no longer walking around on earth, so when I have a question, I just get my answer online or ask my religious friend." Both will give you their opinions, right or wrong. But if you have accepted Jesus Christ as your personal savior, you have the Holy Spirit living inside you. Ask Him.

So why are so many Christians against biblical prosperity? And even more important, what are you telling God when you reject His prosperity? Satan works hard to redefine what God has created into lies and deceptions. Look how Satan has redefined the image of the rainbow. He has perverted it from a prosperity covenant He made with Noah and all future generations into an LGBT symbol. Satan has redefined the meaning of many biblical words, as well, such as *marriage*. In addition, the word *blessing* has been reduced to a nicety after a sneeze, and *prosperity* has been reduced to a get-rich-quick theology.

God not only wants to be our source for every kind of provision, He also wants to abundantly provide for us. Once we know and accept this, we can confidently approach God and ask Him to bless us and bring us into His prosperity. What does the Bible have to say about prosperity?

3 John 2 (AMP) – Beloved, I pray that in every way you may succeed and prosper and be in good health [physically], just as [I know] your soul prospers [spiritually].

Jeremiah 29:11 (NIV) – "For I know the plans I have for you," declares the Lord, "plans to prosper you and not to harm you, plans to give you hope and a future."

Deuteronomy 5:33 (NIV) – Walk in obedience to all that the Lord your God has commanded you, so that you may live and prosper and prolong your days in the land that you will possess.

Deuteronomy 28:11 (NIV) – The Lord will grant you abundant prosperity—in the fruit of your womb, the young of your livestock and the crops of your ground—in the land he swore to your ancestors to give you.

Psalm 1:3 (NIV) – That person is like a tree planted by streams of water, which yields its fruit in season and whose leaf does not wither—whatever they do prospers.

Psalm 128:2 (NIV) – You will eat the fruit of your labor; blessings and prosperity will be yours.

Proverbs 8:18 (NIV) – With me are riches and honor, enduring wealth and prosperity.

Proverbs 11:25 (NIV) – A generous person will prosper; whoever refreshes others will be refreshed.

Proverbs 16:20 (NIV) – Whoever gives heed to instruction prospers, and blessed is the one who trusts in the Lord.

Philippians 4:12 (AMP) – I know how to get along and live humbly [in difficult times], and I also know how to enjoy abundance and live in prosperity. In any and every circumstance I have learned the secret [of facing life], whether well-fed or going hungry, whether having an abundance or being in need.

As you read through the chapters that contain these scriptures on prosperity, you will find that God promises to reward us for obedience.

Hebrews 11:6 (NIV) – And without faith it is impossible to please God, because anyone who comes to him must believe that he exists and that he rewards those who earnestly seek him.

So, the reason so many Christians are against prosperity when there are so many scriptures that clearly promise it is simple: Satan's lies. At some point, these people have asked God to do something for them – get them a new job or more money, heal them of an illness, lead them into new relationships, or show them what their purpose is – and when God didn't do what they wanted, when they wanted, they gave up and lowered their expectation of what God will do for them. They felt burned. Oh they'll admit to you that God *can do* anything because after all, He's sovereign. But it doesn't take a lot of faith to believe God *might do* something for you. It takes great faith, patience, and perseverance, on the other hand, to believe that God will make good on His Word, especially when after much time, He hasn't answered your prayers. Inevitably, they join a camp of believers WHO *might believe* in God; they just don't believe Him or His Word. These are low-faith individuals, many times low-faith intellectuals, who are especially bothered by anyone who has high-faith expectations, or faith expectations higher than theirs.

Sadly, they live beneath their privilege. They can't handle any big assignments from God. Low-faith individuals aim about one inch from their present circumstances and net low results. They don't believe the 6,000-plus promises in the Bible are for them. They've rationalized God's promises and powered down to the peanut size of their faith.

Many are intellectuals produced out of religious seminary institutions, with information but no revelation knowledge. They recite and interpret the Word of God through the lens of their favorite Christian scholars more than the truth of the Holy Spirit. They are spirit deaf. They would rather err on the side of not enough faith than too much. For these folks, some things are possible, just not anything. They believe in God, but they don't believe Jesus when He said:

Mark 9:23 (KJV) – Jesus said unto him, If thou canst believe, all things are possible to him that believeth.

The low-faith individual will reduce this scripture to a flesh-minded philosophy that lacks the power to accomplish its purpose and promise, instead of a faith-producing inspiration of the Holy Spirit.

Colossians 2:8 (NIV) – See to it that no one takes you captive through hollow and deceptive **philosophy**, which depends on human tradition and the elemental spiritual forces of this world rather than on Christ.

Isaiah 55:11 (NIV) – So is my word that goes out from my mouth: It will not return to me empty, but will accomplish what I desire and achieve the purpose for which I sent it.

2 Timothy 3:16-17 (NIV) – All Scripture is God-breathed and is useful for teaching, rebuking, correcting and training in righteousness, so that the servant of God may be thoroughly equipped for every good work.

Anyone experiencing some sort of lack in their life – lack of finances, lack of health, lack of relationship, or lack of purpose, and they begin to read the Bible – IT'S GOOD NEWS. In fact, IT'S GREAT NEWS! When they start reading through the 6,000 or so promises, their hope is renewed. The Bible doesn't have geographic boundaries. There is no place on the planet where God's Word doesn't work. If you live in a poverty area, and you are poor, and you are raised by poor people, and you have poor neighbors, and you lack education or a job, here's the good news. You don't have to wait until the right political party gets into office; you don't have to wait until racial discrimination ends; and you don't have to wait until you get to Heaven. It's God's desire that you prosper right here on earth. It is His will. And if you'll believe Him and follow Him, you can be prosperous. God has a plan and purpose for your life, a plan to prosper you!

Jeremiah 29:11 (NIV) – "For I know the plans I have for you," declares the Lord, "plans to prosper you and not to harm you, plans to give you hope and a future."

No circumstance, no situation, no nothing can stop you from fulfilling God's plan and purpose for your life. God is on your side. If you are part of His family, a Christian, He has forgiven you of ALL sin, past, present, and future. If you are sinning right now, just repent and move forward toward His wonderful prosperity. People who reject God's prosperity spread this lack of hope to other people who really need God to help them. It's a shame. It's vain. It's pride. It's lack of knowledge. It's Satan's grand deception. Don't partner with Satan's lies.

Throughout scripture, we read that nothing is impossible if we would only believe. We need to have faith and believe in His promises for us.

Fear not. Believe only. Everything is possible.

What is the difference between God's provision and God's prosperity? Provision is God's covenant to take care of us, to provide for us. Think of it as a parent's role to provide for his or her children. Good parents put food on the table, clothe their children, and provide shelter. This is God's promise to provide.

Philippians 4:19 (NIV) – And my God will meet all your needs according to the riches of his glory in Christ Jesus.

But prosperity is God's covenant promise to reward us for our good behavior. His plan to prosper us is the result of believing and doing as the Bible instructs. As an example, the phrase *fear not* appears in the Bible around 170 times. Even the slowest learner might conclude that God is trying to tell us something here. The word *faith* appears in the Bible around 336 times. The Bible says God grants prosperity to those who fear not and have faith.

Hebrews 11:6 (NIV) – And without faith it is impossible to please God, because anyone who comes to him must believe that he exists and that he rewards those who earnestly seek him.

Mark 9:23 (NIV) – "'If you can'?" said Jesus. "Everything is possible for one who believes."

Matthew 21:21 (NIV) – Jesus replied, "Truly I tell you, if you have faith and do not doubt, not only can you do what was done to the fig tree, but also you can say to this mountain, "Go, throw yourself into the sea," and it will be done."

Luke 8:50 (NIV) – Hearing this, Jesus said to Jairus, "Don't be afraid; just believe, and she will be healed."

Mark 5:36 (NIV) – Overhearing what they said, Jesus told him, "Don't be afraid; just believe."

Think about these scriptures. First, you can't please God without faith. Everything is possible for those who believe. If everything were possible, what would you stop being afraid to do? What would you stop failing to do? If everything were possible, what would you go after? How big would your dreams be? Would they be as big as our God? How high would you aim if you could fear not, have faith, and believe only. God rewards those who believe Him, those who exercise their faith. Fear tolerated is faith contaminated.

I am a believer of God's prosperity, not man's religion of social justice. I don't look to man for my prosperity; I look to God. If man is unfair, it's doesn't reduce the power of God's promises for prosperity.

Think of the prosperity-minded believer as a faith warrior who aims his or her faith high, based on the power of God's promises, regardless of and oblivious to the perceived impossibility of his or her present circumstances. Faith warriors have a genuine desire to be richly blessed so they can be a blessing to others. These folks see someone in need and cry out "Jehovah-Jireh, the Lord who provides, Jehovah-Rapha, the Lord who heals, bless me, Father, so I can be a blessing to those in need. Make me prosperous, Lord, so I can bring glory to Your Name," as if it was their own personal need. They are generous with their time and money. They look at every need as an opportunity to bring glory to God. They would give you the shirts off their backs. Some have modest incomes and some are rich. But either way their expectation is matched by their faith. Their future is not determined by their present circumstances; it is determined by God's plan and purpose for their lives, no matter how impossible it may seem. These prosperity-minded individuals should be you and me. People who aim high. People empowered by God Himself to do all He has called us to do.

Unfortunately, too many of us fall into the low-faith camp of the poverty-minded Christian. These folks tend to desire only enough for themselves. Both low- and high-income people fall into this trap, most often unintentionally. They are unsure of God's intention to bless us ALL, especially financially. They're not sure how to please God, and as a result, they don't have the faith to believe God's promises. They've never thought to ask God to bless them so they can bless others. Instead they shrug their shoulders in helplessness and hopelessness over other people's sorry situations. They focus on their problems, not on other people's problems. They don't realize God often works through ordinary people like you and me to meet the needs of others. They appear humble, but their prayer life reveals a selfish heart. A stubborn heart. A prideful heart. To them, what's possible is determined by their present circumstances, not by the power of faith in God's Word.

While they believe in social justice, God's power is unfortunately rendered powerless until mankind changes, or the right political power can get into office and force justice upon us. They are blind to the fact that God's kingdom power is in EVERY believer right now. Satan is thrilled. These folks won't do much for the Kingdom unless all the circumstances are just right. And if they hit any obstacles along the way, they're done. Finished. They try, but can't do, because they don't believe.

Prosperity is God's choice for you. Make it yours today.

The Big Idea

Stage 10 - Prosperity:
The High-Faith Believer

STOP! Ask God to wipe clean opinions and thinking that you may have regarding prosperity. Then spend an enormous amount of time searching the scriptures and allowing the Holy Spirit to renew your thinking. Get an aerial view, a God view. You have a choice: lower the bar to match your faith, or raise your faith to match God's bar. Or, you can always fight God with your opinions.

1. Ask God to renew your mind.
2. Fill yourself full of the Word.
3. Allow the Holy Spirit to teach you.

Notes

Conclusion

Congrats! You've now read the Genesis-to-Revelation of *HisPlan MyPlan*. Down deep inside you is a God-sized, God-planted dream. You already know God created you in His very own image to do great things here on earth. Greater things. You were meant to do something greater than what you are doing right now. And you know it!

Let's review: *HisPlan MyPlan* stages are focused on how to identify and fulfill God's plan and purpose for your life.

Stages 1 through 6 are the faith basics. Your faith foundation. Without this foundation, your house will crumble under the pressure from life's storms.

Stage 1 – Inheritance

You believe and receive the inheritance Jesus bought at the cross with His blood and through the resurrection. More than 6,000 promises to empower you through ANY situation.

Stage 2 – Source

As a result of much time invested in the Word and prayer, you have a two-way relationship with God.

Stage 3 – Permission

You have given God permission to change your way of thinking to His way of thinking.

Stage 4 – Learning

As a result of changing your way of thinking to His way, you've also changed your way of doing to His way.

Stage 5 – Battle

You know how to effectively put on the armor of Christ, allowing God, though His Word, to conquer your circumstances for you.

Stage 6 – Faith

You walk by faith, not by doubt.

Stage 7 – Purpose

You know how to approach identifying personal purpose with confidence, expectation, and faith.

Stage 8 – Start

You're taking your first steps of obedience toward your purpose, even when it often seems illogical in the flesh.

Stages 9 and 10 focus on how to aim higher with God-sized goals, trusting Him to provide everything necessary to fulfill His plan.

Stage 9 – Provision

You are trusting God to be your absolute source for everything.

Stage 10 – Prosperity

You are aiming higher with God-sized dreams and goals.

HisPlan MyPlan makes a great checklist for accomplishing your calling. Look at each stage and ask yourself, "How has my thinking, doing, and results changed for the better because of what I've learned in each stage?" If you approach HPMP with both a learner's and a doer's heart, nothing will be impossible for you. I encourage you to visit hisplanmyplan.com for more teaching and events to help you grow and succeed in your journey toward your destiny.

Best,

Gerald Duran

Made in the USA
San Bernardino, CA
10 January 2018